The Heroes
Hailsham

"Lest we forget the men of Hailsham , in Sussex, who died fighting for King and Country"

.... 88 in World War I
....35 in World War II

An illustrated history of Hailsham's War Memorial and a record of the lives and actions of the men of Hailsham, in Sussex, who died for King and Country in both the First (1914–18) and also the Second (1939–45) World Wars and whose names are recorded on the Memorial in the High Street, Hailsham.

Researched and Written by David M. Dyer, BSc(Hons).

Published by DMD Publishing, Davley House, 18 Fairisle Close, Hailsham, E. Sussex, BN27 3HD

Price £9.00

NOTE – Net profits from this book will be donated to the following Service Charities: - British Legion (50%); Thank the Forces (25%).

The Heroes of Hailsham

This edition published in 2011
by DMD Publishing

ISBN 978-0-9569155-0-4

British Library Cataloguing in Publication Data
A catalogue record for this book is available from the British Library

Paperback ISBN 978-0-9569155-0-4

Typeset by the Author on Ariel 11

Printed and bound by CPI Group (UK) Ltd, Croydon, CR0 4YY

Published by DMD Publishing, Davley House, 18 Fairisle Close, Hailsham BN27 3HD

The Heroes of Hailsham

David M. Dyer, BSc(Hons)
Author and Researcher

<u>Cover Illustrations</u> – The photograph of Hailsham's war Memorial shown on the front cover of this book, as shown below, will be readily apparent to all Hailsham residents. The photograph shown on the rear cover of this book, also reproduced below, is, very obviously, of the same war memorial in the High Street but was taken in 1920 when it was first erected. Because of this, many residents will not be familiar with the background scenery. Whilst the war memorial has remained in the same place, the original 'Old Comrades Club' was moved and replaced by the Hailsham Club as part of the late 1960's development of Vicarage Field.

<u>Front Cover</u>

<u>Rear Cover</u>

The Heroes of Hailsham

Dedication

This book is dedicated to my wife, Lesley, a Hailsham person in the true sense of the word, who has provided me with a great deal of local knowledge and useful advice and who has also given me much help and support in producing this book, particularly with the onerous task of proofreading.

About the Author and this Book

About the Author

Having been born and brought up in Bexhill, Dave Dyer has lived in Hailsham since 1968 and regards the history of Hailsham as being important to the town. He has three children, two of whom still live in the area. He has since re-married. He obtained his Bachelor of Science (Honours) Degree in Social Science through the Open University in 2004. Now retired after 42 years in local government, he is busier than ever. He is also well versed in family history research which has proved very useful in researching for this book.

Previous Publications

Previous books researched and written by the Author include: -

"The Lives and Times of the Dyer Family of Alton: 1633 to 1990"
"90 Years of Scouting in Hellingly: 1911 to 2001"
"Bexhill Charter Trustees: Centenary of the Borough Coat of Arms"
"1st Hellingly Scout Group: Centenary History/Programme 2011"

Sources of Reference

It has been quite difficult to undertake this research because of the lack of available information. It is a complete myth that everything can be found on the internet, particularly as, if it is there, so much of it is wrong. The records which would have been made at the time were not kept or, more likely, were used to help the war effort with 'waste paper'. To compound the problem, 'our' Memorial, unlike some others, does not give any information on the Service, Regiment, Rank or age of those who fell. However, other information has been found which has helped lives to be pieced together. The following are the main sources which have been used in this research.

Prime/Original records - mainly via 'Ancestry', 'Find-My-Past', 'Roll-of-Honour' and the Commonwealth War Graves Commission.

Newspapers – Sussex Express & County Herald, Eastbourne Chronicle, Eastbourne Herald

Local Libraries – Eastbourne, Hailsham and Hastings.

National Libraries - National Newspaper Library, Colindale, London

Record Office – East Sussex (at the Maltings, Lewes)

Relatives - Information from relatives. (See list of acknowledgements on page 172)

Museums – Hailsham Museum/Heritage Centre at Blackmans Yard; Redoubt Museum in Eastbourne

Cemetery – Cemetery records held by Hailsham Town Council

Parish magazines - St Mary's Parish magazines - WW I only *(WW II not in existence)*

Table of Contents

Table of Contents (contd)

Part Three – World War II

Part Four – Additional Information

Introduction

The year 2011, marks the 90th anniversary of the erection of the War Memorial in the High Street of Hailsham. This book is published to coincide with this 90th anniversary. The fact that these men gave their lives for King and Country is not a matter to be celebrated, but it is important that their deeds and actions are not to be forgotten. Whilst many inhabitants of the town remember, sometimes only too vividly, the lives of those who died, particularly in the Second World war, there are an even greater number who do not know anything about them. War is a dreadful thing which has dramatic effects on the lives of those involved in any way, whether as wives or husbands, parents, grandparents, relatives, friends or just acquaintances.

Hailsham's WWI Memorial, along with almost every other Memorial in the country, is inscribed with the immortal words *"Their Name Liveth For Evermore"*. It is an unfortunate fact of life that, although the names are still visible from those times so many years ago, details of their lives are not. Memories in the vast majority of cases have faded and descendants have often moved away. Fascinating photographs of soldiers, sailors and airmen from times past, often unnamed and undated, are stored in boxes in attics and there is no-one left to explain who they are or what they represent.

This book sets out to illustrate and outline the lives of the 123 men, who are named on Hailsham's War Memorial. It will attempt to show how these men were connected with the town, what they did for the town and to give some idea of the actions in which they lost their lives. References are made to the various military battles or, in some cases, disasters in which these men were involved and this has been done to give some background to what was happening when the fighting took place. It must be remembered that many of these young men, some scarcely more than boys, had only just left school and some even inflated their ages in a spirit of patriotism.

What constitutes a Hailsham person? Although there were undoubtedly 'rules' for determining whether a person should or should not be named on the Memorial, the reasons for inclusion (or exclusion) are not always clear. There are no records at all for any original 'application forms' for names to be included, if ever there were any such things. Most of the men named were either born in the area or brought up and lived with their families in Hailsham. Some moved into Hailsham at an early stage of their lives whilst others came later on to go to school whilst their parent's worked in the town. All of the 123 men had something to do with Hailsham, even if it was only that close relatives lived in the town.

The scope of this research has been restricted to those whose names appear on the Memorial, those who paid the ultimate sacrifice with their lives and died for King and Country. Whilst the title of the book calls them *"Heroes"*, the Author readily acknowledges that the men who fought for their country and survived to live another day, also have the right to be called *"Heroes"*.

Introduction (Contd)

During this research, it became readily apparent that not every Hailsham person who died fighting for King and Country is named on the war Memorial. Indeed, a look around Hailsham cemetery will show that only six of the fifteen graves maintained by the Commonwealth War Graves Commission, are for those named on the Memorial. There are also names on the Memorial boards in both St Mary's Church and Hailsham Boys School, now Hailsham Community College, which do not appear on the Memorial. There are several obvious reasons for these discrepancies. Sometimes the relatives of these men concerned felt that they were more closely connected with another town and have included their names there. Sometimes relatives did not want their men's names to appear as a constant reminder to them. In other cases, men were still recorded as 'missing' many years afterwards and death had not been confirmed. In one particular instance, after the end of WWII, Hailsham Council refused to have someone's name included despite that person having been born and raised in Hailsham. This particular man had joined the navy in 1938 but went down with his ship in the Battle of Crete in 1941. The reason the Council gave was that he had only been reported as "missing" and his death was still unconfirmed, even some three years after the war had ended.

This book does not set out in any way to glorify war; nor does it attempt to be a history of either of the two wars involved as these are very complex subjects fully covered by a multitude of specialised books. What it hopes to do is to fill in a missing gap, an unwritten part of the knowledge that should be available to the town and, as such, is an important part of the history of the town of Hailsham.

ฒฒฒฒฒฒฒฒฒฒ

Footnote 1 - The Author wishes to acknowledge, with grateful thanks, the kind generosity of Hailsham Town Council in supporting this project and sponsoring much of the direct research costs for this book.

Footnote 2 – The information contained in this book is the result of the Author's own research and the official records that exist. This has been supplemented by the many photographs and memories of relatives and descendants. It is accepted that there are some missing gaps in the information produced and that there might be a few inaccuracies. it is hoped that anyone with further information will contact the Author so that this can be recorded for future generations or possibly as a Supplement to this book. Thank you.

ฒฒฒฒฒฒฒฒฒฒ

Message from the Town Mayor

Hailsham
TOWN COUNCIL

Hailsham Town Council
Inglenook, Market Street
Hailsham
East Sussex
BN27 2AE

T: (01323) 841702
F: (01323) 842978
E: enquiries@hailsham-tc.gov.uk

www.hailsham-tc.gov.uk

Town Clerk:
Elizabeth G. Jones

Town Mayor & Chairman:
Councillor Jeff Bentley-Astor

Telephone: 01323 841332
Email: bentlleyastor@sky.com

To: Mr DAVID DYER

Date: MONDAY 8th AUGUST 2011

Dear Mr Dyer,

As an essential feature of the town's identity, the Hailsham War Memorial is passed by many people each day - most of whom have no knowledge of who the people listed on the monument are or what they did before they fought in the two World Wars and gave their lives serving our country. To erect a war memorial in the High Street listing their names was a very worthy project and, apart from the men commemorated on the Hailsham War Memorial, there is a need to create another source whereby people can remember and share details of the casualties of these major conflicts.

Your new book, which uncovers the stories behind the names commemorated on the Hailsham War Memorial, how old they were and what their connection to the local community was, is truly fascinating and helps to bring the war memorial to life. A wide range of interesting stories concerning the lives and actions of these brave heroes has been uncovered and placed in the context of our great town. The book focuses on the individuals rather then the actual battles within the First and Second World Wars, as it was ultimately family members who had to deal with the loss of those commemorated.

This is an admirable book, which has rightfully achieved its aim of raising the profile of our war memorial. It should be of particular value to those at home and abroad who are researching their roots.

Hailsham Town Council has happily assisted you with this important project, and I feel that it is fitting that those who sacrificed their lives should be commemorated in this way. We should never forget the work that these soldiers have done.

Councillor Jeff Bentley-Astor
Town Mayor & Chairman

TWINNED WITH

GOURNAY
en Bray

QUALITY
TOWN
COUNCIL
QC-04-09-00688

Part One – Hailsham Memorials

"Memorials around Hailsham"

The main focus of this first section is to give details of the well-known War Memorial in the High Street. It will set out the reasons why and how it was built where it was and the factors that brought this into existence. This section also shows that there are other Memorials in the Town mainly dedicated to those who died in the Great War although these serve different purposes.

Many people will know that there is a Memorial board on the wall in St Mary's Parish Church. Others might know that there is a similar board in the original Hailsham Council Boys School, now known as Hailsham Community College. The names on these two, however, differ from those names on the High Street Memorial as will be illustrated later. There are also two Memorial tablets in Hailsham Methodist Church dedicated to those who died in both wars and were members of their congregation. The final 'Memorial' is a manual record book maintained by Messrs Burfield & Sons whose rope and twine factory was a major employer in the Town at the time of the Great War.

In addition, there are fifteen war graves in Hailsham Cemetery, which are maintained by the Commonwealth War Graves Commission (Ten for WW I and five for WW II). However, only six of these (five for WW I and one for WW II) are for those named on the High Street War Memorial. There are also other war service and civilian war death graves in the Cemetery but these are private graves, paid for by the families. Various memorial inscriptions to those who died in both wars are also to be found around the Hailsham Cemetery.

ഇഇഇഇഇഇഇഇഇഇഇ

Part One – Hailsham Memorials

<u>High Street War Memorial</u>

Peace was declared and the Armistice was signed on 11th November 1918. 17 days later, on 28th November 1918, Hailsham Parish Council resolved to: -

".... take the initiative for providing by public subscription a permanent memorial for the men of Hailsham who made the supreme sacrifice in the great world war whilst serving in His Majesty's Forces upholding the cause of Freedom and Justice ...."

The first public meeting held on 8th January 1919 discussed the Parish Council recommendations of how best the town could express their respect and gratitude for those who died in the Great War. The meeting agreed to attempt to carry out three proposals:- (1) That a monument, together with a memorial hall, be erected in the High Street; (2) That 'South View' in Western Road, opposite the Recreation Ground, should be purchased for conversion into a public library and institute, & (3) That an Institute be provided for returned servicemen and Hailsham inhabitants to meet socially.

The original look of the war Memorial before the addition of the dedication to those who fell in the Second World War.

While efforts were being made to raise the money, a letter was sent by two brothers, J.Robert Green and Arthur Green, offering to purchase the house and present it to the Council in memory of their brother, Ewart Victor Green, who was killed in action at

8

High Street War Memorial (contd)

Poelcapelle, in Belgium, north of Lille on 30th October 1917. The acceptance of the gift was confirmed by the council on 14th November 1919 when it was agreed the house be converted into a library with a reading room and an 'institute' for recreation. In April 1920, the library was opened together with a Memorial Institute that had a games room with a billiard table. The library was under the supervision of two honorary librarians and with a total of seven hundred and fifty books, one hundred and ninety six people were enrolled. The cost of furnishing both the library and the reading room was a little over £100.

The council meeting held on 28th November 1918 had also favoured the erection of a monument to the fallen together with a war memorial hall somewhere in the High Street. Once again, a fine gesture solved this second public approved plan, for a Mr J.S.O. Robertson-Luxford offered a suitable plot of land to the council. The land next to the old chestnut tree in the High Street was accepted and a grey Cornish granite war Memorial was erected. It was 'unveiled' on 28th November 1920 by Lord Leconfield, who was then the Lord Lieutenant of the County of Sussex.

The unveiling programme   **Packed crowds at the unveiling ceremony**

Later in the same year, the rest of the land behind the war memorial was let by the Council to the 'Comrades of the Great War' at a rent of 5s.0d per year and on the site was built a wooden memorial hut named the 'Old Comrades Club'.

The war Memorial takes the form of a wheel cross with celtic-style relief on the head and down the shaft of the cross. This cross is set on a stone plinth with four tablets attached bearing the names in black lettering of 88 Hailsham men who died in the First World War.

Part One – Hailsham Memorials

High Street War Memorial (contd)

The whole monument is set on a three-stepped base. In addition, there is a stone on one side, which bears the names of the 35 men who fell in the Second World War. This is now set in a low metal surround.

At first glance, the names of those who fell in the Great War, appear to be in alphabetical order. However, a closer look clearly indicates that some names were added at a later stage and it is interesting to investigate the reasons. When the Memorial was originally unveiled in November 1920, there were only 77 men named on it. This was confirmed by the report in the Sussex Express newspaper, which listed all 77 names. An explanation is now given for the other 11 names which were added later.

The main reason for this is that some of them died, mainly of their wounds, after the engraving had been completed. This would include: - Joseph Levett (*d. July 1920*), Alfred Lusted (*d.* Mar *1922*) and Wilfred Maryan (*d. May 1922*). There are a further six names, which were not included for various reasons: - Herbert Funnell, James Harriott, Charles Hollibone, Frederick Matthews, Ernest Pelling and Thomas Rigglesford, none of which were shown on St Mary's Church Memorial board. What is somewhat surprising is that the names of Nelson V. Carter, VC and T.C.J. Marillier, DCM, two of our most decorated soldiers, were not shown on the original Memorial, even though they were named on St Mary's Church Memorial board. No explanation has been found for this.

෴෴෴෴෴෴෴෴෴෴

WAR MEMORIAL, HAILSHAM

Flowers adorning Hailsham's war Memorial after the unveiling ceremony in 1920.
Note the absence of any shops in the background compared with the present day

Part One – Hailsham Memorials

High Street War Memorial (contd)

The four tablets naming those who died in the Great War

North Face (25 names)

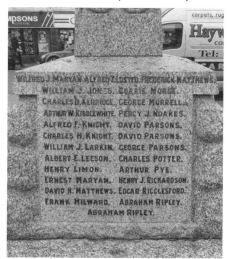

West Face (12 names)

South Face (25 names)

East Face (26 names)

High Street War Memorial (contd)

The 88 men named on the High Street Memorial (in alphabetical order)		
Alderton, Frederick	**H**arvey, Richard Ernie	**P**ye, Arthur
Atkins, Ernest W.	**H**arvey, Rollo D'Aubigne	**R**ichardson, Henry J.
Barber, Robert W.	**H**ollebon, Charles	**R**igglesford, Edgar
Bergan, Otto F.	**H**ollebone, Charles	**R**igglesford, T.E.
Boniface, George	**H**ollibone, Henry W.	**R**ipley, Abraham
Boniface, Louis H.	**J**ackson, Robert H.	**R**ipley, Abraham
Boniface, Martin J.	**J**ones, William J.	**R**ipley, George
Brook, James T.	**K**erridge, Charles D.	**S**aunders, Charles
Butler, Frederick	**K**ibblewhite, Arthur W.	**S**aunders, Ernest
Butler, Richard C.	**K**night, Alfred F.	**S**aunders, John
Carter, Nelson V., **VC**	**K**night, Charles H.	**S**eamer, Frederick J.
Charles, William	**L**arkin, William J.	**S**haw, Edward L.
Colarossi, Gilbert	**L**eeson, Albert E.	**S**mith, Frank C.
Colbran, Charles	**L**evett, Joseph R.	**S**mith, George
Cousens, Alfred S.	**L**imon, Henry	**S**mith, John
Cox, Herbert	**L**usted, Alfred T.	**S**mith, Samuel
Davis, Thomas	**M**arrillier, F.C.J., **DCM**	**S**mith, Thomas H.
Deacon, Frederick	**M**aryan, Ernest	**S**tickland, Alfred A.
Divall, Charles H.	**M**aryan, Wilfred J.	**T**ingley, John H.
Elphick, Walter	**M**atthews, Frederick K.	**T**oye, Claude L.
Firrell, Frank	**M**atthews, David H.	**V**ine, Bert
Fox, William	**M**ilward, Frank	**V**ine, James Uriah
Funnell, Herbert L.	**M**orse, Corrie	**W**alker, Arthur
Gadd, James G.	**M**urrell, George	**W**alker, Percy E.
Gater, Ernest R.	**N**oakes, Percy J.	**W**illard, Albert E.
Goad, Charles S.	**P**arsons, David	**W**ood, Frank
Green, Ewart Victor	**P**arsons, David	**W**ood, John
Gunter, John	**P**arsons, George	**W**oodhams, Albert J.
Hall, Jack	**P**elling, Ernest A.	
Harriott, James	**P**otter, Charles	

Part One – Hailsham Memorials

Hailsham Methodist Church

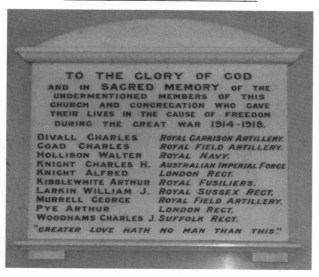

TO THE GLORY OF GOD
AND IN SACRED MEMORY OF THE
UNDERMENTIONED MEMBERS OF THIS
CHURCH AND CONGREGATION WHO GAVE
THEIR LIVES IN THE CAUSE OF FREEDOM
DURING THE GREAT WAR 1914-1918.

DIVALL CHARLES	ROYAL GARRISON ARTILLERY.
GOAD CHARLES	ROYAL FIELD ARTILLERY.
HOLLIBON WALTER	ROYAL NAVY.
KNIGHT CHARLES H.	AUSTRALIAN IMPERIAL FORCE
KNIGHT ALFRED	LONDON REGT.
KIBBLEWHITE ARTHUR	ROYAL FUSILIERS.
LARKIN WILLIAM J.	ROYAL SUSSEX REGT.
MURRELL GEORGE	ROYAL FIELD ARTILLERY.
PYE ARTHUR	LONDON REGT.
WOODHAMS CHARLES J.	SUFFOLK REGT.

"GREATER LOVE HATH NO MAN THAN THIS."

This Memorial board illustrated above is located inside the Hailsham Methodist Church (*formerly the Hailsham Weslyan Church*), in the High Street, Hailsham and commemorates the ten members of the Methodist Church congregation, who died in the First World War. Unlike the other Memorial boards, this one also shows the Regiment in which they served. It was unveiled on 8 August 1920 by Rev Edwin Lansdown, the Superintendent Minister of the Eastbourne Weslyan circuit, using a special form of service for the occasion on which he was also giving his farewell address.

The Sussex Express newspaper reported that: - "*the large congregation stood as the Circuit Superintendent read out the names of the fallen men and he then drew aside the Union Jack covering the tablet*". The impressive service concluded with the singing of the National Anthem.

The names are easily read from the illustration and so are not repeated. However, there is an anomaly in one of the names, that of Charles J. Woodhams. This is the first reference in Hailsham to someone of that name who died in the war. Further research shows that the name of Charles John Woodhams (*which was the name actually read out in the Church service*) actually refers to Albert John Woodhams who served in the Suffolk Regiment. The most logical explanation for this difference is that Albert must have used the name of Charles to distinguish himself from his father, who was also called Albert.

ഇഇഇഇഇഇഇഇഇഇ

Part One – Hailsham Memorials

<u>High Street War Memorial – World War II</u>

1939   OUR GRATITUDE IS   1945
GIVEN ALSO TO THOSE BRAVE
SONS OF HAILSHAM WHO DIED
TO VINDICATE THE SACRIFICE
OF THEIR FATHERS.
WE SHALL ALWAYS REMEMBER :-
EDWARD A. BAYLEY.   KENNETH T. W. MITCHELL.
CLEMENT M. BEARDMORE. FREDERICK J. MOORE.
JACK BONIFACE.   THOMAS H. NEWNHAM.
CHARLES T. BROOK.   ALFRED J. PERRIN.
EDWARD E. BROWN.   HERBERT PETTIGREW.
FRANK A. ERRIDGE.   WILLIAM P. PIPER.
LEONARD F. FEARS.   ERIC F. RAWLINGS.
MICHAEL P. FITZGERALD. REGINALD REYNOLDS.
MARK FULLER.   JOHN H. W. ROBINS.
KENNETH C. FUNNELL. FRANK C. RUSSELL.
MAURICE E. HAFFENDEN. CHARLES W. SARGENT.
RAYMOND A. HELSDON. ALAN B. R. SAUNDERS.
HENRY HIDE.   HENRY T. SEA-MAYS.
ROBIN JARVIS.   ALBERT J. SKINNER.
HERMAN J. KAUTER.   WILLIAM F. C. STAPLEY.
GEORGE E. KING.   FREDK W. STONESTREET.
WALTER LANGLEY.   NORMAN J. WAKEHAM.
WILFRED A. LOVELL.

The plaque commemorating those who died in World War II

This shows the iron railings which are a later addition to the Memorial

In September 1944, even before the end of the war, a public meeting was held to come up with suitable ideas for a memorial in Hailsham for those who had been killed. There were three suggestions, namely: - a cottage hospital, a public hall and a community centre. Hailsham Parish Council appointed a sub-committee to consider the three suggestions and also for the design of the addition to the war memorial for the names of those who fell.

In January 1947, the wardens of the war memorial were empowered to have the names of those from the parish who gave their lives to be inscribed on the monument. Six months later, the wardens decided on the final design, which had been drawn up by a local resident, 'Bill' Brook, for a stone slab at the base of the monument. They pointed out that the council could not meet the cost and that it must be paid for by voluntary effort. In April 1948, instructions were given to the stone masons to inscribe the names of the fallen. The eventual dedication did not take place until just over 18 months later.

The ceremony of dedicating the memorial tablet took place on Remembrance Day in November 1949. Those who assembled included relatives and friends of the fallen of both wars, members of the Parish Council and representatives of organisations in the

Part One – Hailsham Memorials

<u>High Street War Memorial – World War II (contd)</u>

town together with the standards of the British Legion and the flags of the Scouts and Cubs. The British Legion band accompanied the singing of the hymns. The brief service was conducted by the Vicar, the Rev. M.C. Chapman, who dedicated the memorial tablet with the words: -

"To the Glory of God and in grateful and loving memory of the men of Hailsham who gave their lives for their country in the world war 1939-45, we dedicate this memorial stone on which their names are graven, proud of their fidelity, honouring their valour and mourning their loss."

Rev. Leslie Robinson, Hailsham Methodist Minister, then gave an address. This was followed by the two minutes silence, the "Last Post" and the British Legion exhortation "They shall grow not old," recited by the Rev. Robinson and followed by "Reveille".

Regarding the other three suggestions put forward four years earlier, by February 1948 the British Legion were getting restless as nothing appeared to be happening. The branch chairman pointed out that proposals put forward at various times included an obelisk, a cottage hospital, a swimming pool and a memorial hall but the general opinion appeared to be in favour of a hall. The Parish Council considered that the Legion's plans were too ambitious and called another public meeting. In May 1948, a parish meeting held at the Corn Exchange adopted the suggestions put forward by the Legion of a memorial in the form of a community or social centre although it was realised that a considerable sum would be involved and that it would be many years before the project could be completed. It was not until the early 1980s, that the Community Centre was finally built in Vicarage Lane, financed mainly by public subscription.

கு கு கு கு கு கு கு கு கு கு கு

Bayley, Edward A.	Hide, Henry	Rawlings, Eric F.
Beardmore, Clament M.	Jarvis, Robin	Reynolds, Reginald
Boniface, Jack	Kauter, Herman J.	Robins, John H.W.
Brook, Charles T.	King, George E.	Russell, Frank C.
Brown, Edward E.	Langley, Walter	Sargent, Charles W.
Erridge, Frank A.	Lovell, Wilfred A.	Saunders, Alan B.R.
Fears, Leonard F.	Mitchell, Kenneth T.W.	Sea-Mays, Henry T.
Fitzgerald, Michael P.	Moore, Frederick J.	Skinner, Albert J.
Fuller, Mark	Newnham, Thomas H.	Stapley, William F.C.
Funnell, Kenneth G.	Perrin, Alfred J.	Stonestreet, Fredk W.
Haffenden, Maurice E.	Pettigrew, Herbert	Wakeham, Norman J.
Helsdon, Raymond A.	Piper, William P.	

Part One – Hailsham Memorials

St Mary's Parish Church, Hailsham

FREDERICK ALDERTON.	JOHN GUNTER.	CHARLES POTTER.
ERNEST W. ATKINS.	JACK HALL.	ARTHUR PYE.
ROBERT W. BARBER.	RICHARD ERNLE HARVEY.	HENRY JESSE RICHARDSON.
OTTO F. BERGAN.	ROLLO D'AUBIGNE HARVEY.	EDGAR RIGGLESFORD.
GEORGE BONIFACE.	JAMES HARRIOTT.	THOMAS E. RIGGLESFORD.
LOUIS H. BONIFACE.	CHARLES HOLLEBON.	ABRAHAM RIPLEY.
MARTIN J. BONIFACE.	CHARLES HOLLEBONE.	ABRAHAM RIPLEY.
JAMES T. BROOK.	HENRY W. HOLLIBONE.	GEORGE RIPLEY.
FREDERICK BUTLER.	ROBERT H. JACKSON.	CHARLES SAUNDERS.
RICHARD CHAS. BUTLER.	WILLIAM J. JONES.	ERNEST SAUNDERS.
NELSON VICTOR CARTER. V.C.	CHARLES D. KERRIDGE.	JOHN SAUNDERS. M.M.
WILLIAM CHARLES.	ARTHUR W. KIBBLEWHITE.	FREDERICK J. SEAMER.
GILBERT COLAROSSI.	ALFRED F. KNIGHT.	EDWARD L. SHAW.
CHARLES COLBRAN.	CHARLES H. KNIGHT.	FRANK C. SMITH.
THOS WILLIAM COLEMAN.	WILLIAM JOHN LARKIN.	GEORGE SMITH.
ERNEST EDMUND COLEMAN.	ALBERT E. LEESON.	JOHN SMITH.
ALFRED STANLEY COUSENS.	JOSEPH R. LEVETT.	SAMUEL SMITH.
HERBERT COX.	HENRY LIMON.	THOMAS HENRY SMITH.
THOMAS DAVIS.	F.C.J. MARILLIER. D.C.M.	ALFRED A. STICKLAND.
FREDERICK DEACON.	ERNEST MARYAN	JOHN H. TINGLEY.
CHARLES HENRY DIVALL.	DAVID H. MATTHEWS.	CLAUDE L. TOYE.
WALTER ELPHICK.	FRANK MILWARD.	BERT VINE.
FRANK FIRRELL.	CORRIE MORSE.	JAMES URIAH VINE.
WILLIAM FOX.	GEORGE MURRELL.	ARTHUR WALKER.
HERBERT L. FUNNELL.	PERCY J. NOAKES.	PERCY E. WALKER.
JAMES GEORGE GADD.	DAVID PARSONS.	ALBERT E. WILLARD.
ERNEST ROWLAND GATER.	DAVID PARSONS.	FRANK WOOD.
CHARLES S. GOAD.	GEORGE PARSONS.	JOHN WOOD.
EWART VICTOR GREEN.	ERNEST A. PELLING.	ALBERT J. WOODHAMS.

THOSE WHO FELL IN THE GREAT WAR.

On the wall inside St Mary's Church, Hailsham is another Memorial board commemorating Hailsham's war dead from World War I. This board was dedicated at the Memorial Service held at St Mary's Church on 29th December 1919. There are a total of 87 names on this board whereas there are 88 names on the War Memorial in the High Street. The names of three men shown on the High Street Memorial (*Alfred Lusted, Wilfred Maryan and Frederick Matthews*) are not shown on this board. However, two men (*Thos William Coleman and Ernest Edmund Coleman*) are on this board but do not appear of the High Street Memorial.

Before the Memorial board was erected, a request was made for details of the men who died to be sent in to the Church. The 'Roll of Honour' (*see over*) was printed in the Parish Magazine at the end of 1919. Each of the names was read out at the Memorial Service held on 29th December 1919 by Mr C.F. Towler, A.C.P. It is interesting that this list, which shows a total of 88 names, includes many that do not appear either on the Memorial in the Church nor on the Memorial board in Hailsham Council Boys School.

St Mary's Parish Church, Hailsham (contd)

ROLL OF HONOUR.

Names of Men of the Parish of Hailsham, or "Old Boys" of the Hailsham Council Boys' School who fell during the Great War, 1914—1918.

Rank.	Name.	Regiment.
Sergt.	E. W. Atkins	Royal Sussex
Pte.	Fred. Alderton	Canadian Pioneers
,,	J. T. Brooks	A.S.C.
,,	Fred. Burgess	Royal Sussex
,,	A. Barnard	Canadian M.G.C.
,,	Louis H. Boniface	2nd Suffolks
,,	Martin J. Boniface	Royal Sussex
Cpl.	Robt. H. G. Butcher	,,
Pte.	R. L. Butcher	5th Royal Fusiliers
,,	Robt. W. Barber	Queen's R. W. Surrey
,,	Geo. Boniface	7th Royal Fusiliers
Seaman	Frederic Butler	H.M.S. Good Hope
Sapper	R. C. Butler	R.E.
C.S.M.	Wm. Thos. Coleman	Royal Sussex
Pte.	Edmund Coleman	,,
,,	Gilbert Colarossi	,,
Gnr.	Wm. Charles	R.F.A.
C.S.M.	Nelson Victor Carter, V.C.	R. Sussex
Dvr.	Alf. S. Cousins	R.F.A.
Bdr.	Fredk. Coleman	R.G.A.
Pte.	Walter Crosby	Canadian Infantry
Cpl.	Fredk. Deacon	6th Buffs
Pte.	Thos. Davis	M.G.C.
,,	Walter Elphick	Royal Sussex
Lce.-Cpl.	Frank Firrell	,,
Pte.	Ernest Rowland Gates	M.G.C.
Rfm.	Ewart V. Green	London Rifle Bgde.
Dvr.	Chas. S. Goad	R.F.A.
Pte.	Jas. Geo. Gadd	Royal Sussex
Capt. & Adjutant	Richard Ernle Harvey	9th Black Watch
Capt.	Rollo D'Aubigné Harvey	Royal Sussex
Pte.	Chas. Hollebone	,,
Cpl.	Alf. H. Hastings, M.M. with Bar	16th Canadian Scottish
Seaman	Hy. W. Hollibone	H.M.S. Laforey
Pte.	Wm. Geo. Hearsey	Royal Sussex
,,	Jack Hall	,,
Lce.-Cpl.	Robt. Harold Jackson	,,
Pte.	Wm. J. Jones	11th ,,
,,	Charles D. Kerridge	Artists Rifles
,,	Ar. W. Kibblewhite	Royal Fusiliers
Rfm.	Alf. F. Knight	17th London Rifles
Cpl.	Chas. H. Knight	Australians
Pte.	Tom Kemp	Royal Sussex
,,	Henry Limon	H.A.C.
,,	William John Larkin	Royal Sussex

Rank.	Name.	Regiment.
Lieut.	F. C. Jennings Marillier, D.C.M.	Royal Sussex
Pte.	Corrie Morse	Royal Fusiliers
Gnr.	Alf. Miller	R.H.A.
Pte.	Geo. Miller	Middlesex
Sergt.	Geo. Murrell	R.F.A.
Pte.	Ernest Maryan	2nd Royal Sussex
,,	David Matthews	,,
,,	E. V. Message	Grenadier Guards
,,	Percy J. Noakes	9th Royal Sussex
,,	David Parsons	5th ,,
,,	Arthur Pye	7th City of London
,,	George Parsons	2nd R.M.L.I.
Seaman	Fred. Robins	H.M.S. Good Hope
Sergt.	Harold Rapson	
Pte.	Edgar Rigglesford	2nd Royal Sussex
Sergt.	Robert H. Roberts	11th ,,
Pte.	Abraham Ripley	4th Middlesex
Cpl.	,, ,,	Royal Fusiliers
Pte.	Hy. Jesse Richardson	13th London Rgt.
2nd Lieut.	Edward Lockhart Shaw	Queen's Royal W. Surrey
Pte.	Fredk. J. Seamer	Coldstream Guards
Sergt.	John Saunders, M.M. and Serbian Gold Medal	R.H.A.
Pte.	Tom Smith	A.S.C.
,,	Geo. Smith	2nd Royal Sussex
,,	Chas. Harold Smith	1st Sx. Yeomanry
,,	John Smith	Duke of Cornwall's L.I.
,,	Samuel Smith	Royal Sussex
,,	A. A. Stickland	13th ,,
,,	Fredk. Stevens	Labour Corps
,,	Ernest Saunders	Suffolks
,,	Charles Saunders	9th Royal Fusiliers
,,	C. L. Toye	Royal Sussex
Rfm.	John Tingley	Rifle Brigade
Gnr.	Jas. U. Vine	R.F.A.
Pte.	Bert Vine	5th Royal Sussex
Lieut.	A. E. Willard	,,
Pte.	H. G. Woodhams	Royal West Surrey
Gnr.	E. Woodhams	R.G.A.
1st Class P.O.	John Wood	H.M.S. Flirt
Cpl.	Frank Wood	2/6th Royal Warwicks
Pte.	Albert J. Woodhams	2nd Suffolks
,,	Percy E. Walker	Royal Sussex
,,	Arthur Walker	,,

The Roll of Honour was read by Mr. C. F. Towler, A.C.P., December 29th, at the Memorial Service in the Parish Church.

Part One – Hailsham Memorials

Hailsham Council Boys School

In the Reception area of what is now Hailsham Community College, there is a Memorial board, which shows a total of 82 names and ranks of those who died in the Great War and were connected with the school. All of the 82 are former pupils of the school except for two who were teachers. However, of those only 60 are actually named on the High Street Memorial as they are possibly commemorated elsewhere.

The School Log Book records the following. *"Lt. Col. C W Owen, CMG, CIE, JP. (Chairman of the Hailsham group of Council School Managers) undertook the ceremony of unveiling the Memorial Tablet on Aug 1st 1919. This Memorial was erected to the memory of the Old Boys of the school who had fallen during the Great War. It was subscribed to by the scholars & staff of the Boys school, the staff of the Girls school, the Visiting Managers, Mr Firrell, Mr & Mrs C F Towler, Mrs Atkins, Mr & Mrs A. Hillman, Mrs Guy & Mrs A. Willard."*

It is also recorded that Mr Alfred Thornton kindly gave the marble, which he cut and polished and fixed in position and that the lettering was cut by an 'old boy' of the school (Mr E Thornton) who *"only charged for his time (sic)"*.

൸൸൸൸൸൸൸൸൸൸

Hailsham Council Boys School (contd)

Pte	Alderton, F.	*	Pte	Gates, E.R.	*	Pte	Richardson, H.J.	*
Sergt	Atkins, E.W.	*	Dvr	Goad, C.S.	*	Pte	Rigglesford, E.	*
Pte	Barber, R.W.	*	Pte	Hall, J.	*	Cpl	Ripley, A.	*
Pte	Barnard, A.		Cpl	Hastings, A.,		Pte	Ripley, A.	*
Pte	Boniface, G.	*		**MM with Bar**		Pte	Ripley, G.	*
Pte	Boniface, L.H.	*	Pte	Hearsey, W.C.		Sergt	Roberts, R.H.	
Pte	Boniface, M.J.	*	Pte	Hollebone, C.	*	Pte	Robins, C.E.	
Pte	Brooks, J.T.	*	Seaman	Hollibone, H.W.	*	Seaman	Robins, F.	
Pte	Burgess, F.		L.Cpl	Jackson, R.H.	*	Pte	Saunders, C.	*
Cpl	Butcher, R.H.C.		Pte	Jones, W.J.	*	Pte	Saunders, E.	*
Seaman	Butler, F.	*	Pte	Kemp, T.		Sergt	Saunders, J. **MM**	*
Sapp	Butler, R.C.	*	Pte	Kenny, F.		Pte	Seamer, F.J.	*
CSM	Carter, N.V., **VC**	*	Rfm	Kerridge, C.D.	*	Tpr	Smith, C.H.	
Pte	Colarossi, C.	*	Pte	Kibblewhite, A.W.	*	Pte	Smith, G.	*
Pte	Coleman, E.		Rfm	Knight, A.F.	*	Pte	Smith, J.	*
Bdr	Coleman, F.		Cpl	Knight, C.H.	*	Pte	Smith, S.	*
CSM	Coleman, W.T.		Lieut	Marillier F.C.J. **DCM**	*	Pte	Smith, T.	*
Dvr	Cousins, A.S.		Pte	Maryan, E.	*	Pte	Stickland, A.A.	*
Pte	Cox, H.	*	Pte	Matthews, D.	*	Pte	Vine, E.	*
Pte	Crosby, W.		Pte	Milward, F.	*	Pte	Walker, A.	*
Pte	Davis, T.	*	Pte	Morse, C.	*	Pte	Walker, P.E.	
Cpl	Deacon, F.	*	Sergt	Murrell, G.	*	Lieut	Willard, A.E.	*
Pte	Divall, C.H.	*	Pte	Noakes, P.J.	*	Cpl	Wood, F.	
Pte	Elphick, W.	*	Pte	Parsons, C.		PO	Wood, J.	*
L.Cpl	Firrell, F.	*	Pte	Parsons, D.	*	Pte	Woodhams, A.J.	*
Pte	Foord, W.		Pte	Parsons, D.	*	Gnr	Woodhams, E.	
Pte	Fox, W.	*	Pte	Pye, A.	*	Pte	Woodhams, H.G.	
Pte.	Gadd, J.G.	*	Lieut	Rapson, H.				

*The * shown above indicates that this person is named on the High Street Memorial*

Part One – Hailsham Memorials

Burfield & Son – Rope and Twine Factory

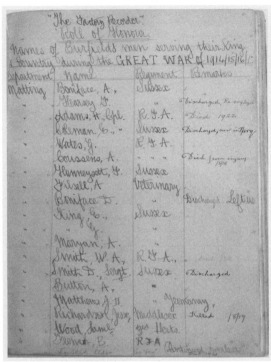

Burfield & Son Limited advertised themselves as manufacturers of rope, line, twine, tarpaulin, rick cloths, corn and coal sacks, cocoa nut mats and matting, hop pocketing, bin bagging, hair cloth, brushes and brooms. They were a major employer in Hailsham at the time of the Great War. Hailsham's 'Rope Museum' is currently housed at Michelham Priory and this includes some fascinating archive records. One of these is Burfield's Factory Record & Visitors book, 1901 to 1926. In this, under the heading of "The Factory Recorder", is a 'Roll of Honour' for Burfield's employees who served in the First World War. Whilst this is not strictly a Memorial, as can be seen from the page illustrated here, it is a record of their names, the department where they worked in the factory, the regiment that they enlisted into and any subsequent remarks. There are four pages in all, the final one showing the names of those who attested under the "Lord Derby" scheme together with the reason that they were not accepted.

The table given below shows the details of those who were working at Burfield's when they were either called up or volunteered, who gave their lives for King and Country and are commemorated on Hailsham's War Memorial.

Department	Name	Regiment	Remarks
Matting	Coussens, A.	R.F.A.	Died from injury - / 8/18
- do -	Richardson, Jesse	Middlesex	Killed - / 8/17
- do -	Lusted, Alf	"Sx - Yes"(*sic*)	Died 1921
Not shown	Maryan, W.J.	R.F.A.	Died 17/ 6/1922
- do -	Fox, Wm	Attached R.E.	*Nil*
- do -	Herriott, J.	*Not shown*	Died 29/10/18
Twine	Levett, J.	Sussex	Died 1921
- do -	Vine, B.	Sussex	Killed - / - /17
- do -	Wood, F.A.	Sussex	Killed - / - /18

Ꭶ Ꭶ Ꭶ Ꭶ Ꭶ Ꭶ Ꭶ Ꭶ Ꭶ Ꭶ

Part Two – The Great War: 1914-18

"Details of the Fallen – WW I"

The following section provides a brief glimpse into the personal lives and military careers of the 88 men whose names are commemorated on Hailsham's War Memorial in the High Street. It also explores the connections that these men had with Hailsham although these have not always been easy to ascertain. Whilst the majority were either born or brought up in the town or were living or working in or near the town before the war, other factors have sometimes come into play to connect these men with Hailsham.

In compiling these records, information has been gained from such sources as census records, particularly 1901 and 1911, St Mary's Church parish magazines, Hailsham Council Boys School records (*almost non-existent*), military service records and other Memorial boards as well as, in some cases, personal knowledge and photographs kindly given and shared by descendants of their families. It is unfortunate that the records, which were made at the time, such as those that would show the justification for the inclusion of names on the memorial and the connection they had with Hailsham, are no longer in existence.

Part Two – The Great War: 1914-18

Alderton, Frederick

Rank	Regiment	Age at Death
Private	Canadian Pioneers	20

Frederick Alderton was born in May 1895. In the 1901 census, Frederick Alderton, aged 5 years old, is shown as being a "*boarder*" at 17 North Street, Hailsham, the home of Fred & Clara Simmons. His birthplace is given as "*not known*" and the probable reason for this will become apparent. Anyway, he was brought up with the Simmons family in Hailsham and went to school in Hailsham for a while. At age 10 years, along with many other '*Home Children*', records show that he was aboard the ship "*Dominion*" which arrived at Montreal, Canada on 12 August 1905, probably as part of the Dr Barnado's emigration scheme whereby workhouse children were sent to Canada under the child labour scheme. In 1906, he is on the Canadian census in a township in Saskatchewan, shown as being a 'hired hand' to the head of the house. On 12 August 1915, at Regina in Saskatchewan, he enlisted into the Canadian Pioneers where he served as a Private (*Service No: 104109*) with the 3rd Battalion. The Regiment undertook war training in England before embarking to France.

In 1916, St Mary's parish magazine carried the following announcement: -

"*Private Fred Alderton (Canadian Pioneers) of Hailsham was shot through the heart in France, April 18th. He was nearly 21 years of age*"

The date of 18th April 1916 was shortly before the Second Battle of Ypres. Frederick was buried at Menin Road South Military Cemetery (*Grave: I.H.28*) in Belgium.

The name and rank of "*Private F. Alderton*" appears on the Memorial board at Hailsham Boys School. His name also appears on the Memorial board in St Mary's Church, Hailsham as well as in the 'Roll of Honour' printed in the parish magazine.

Frederick's military Attestation papers show that he was the son of Frederick and Louisa Alderton, of 36 Mill Road, Bury St Edmunds, in Suffolk. In the 1911 census, whilst Frederick himself was in Saskatchewan, Canada, his parents and a three-year-old brother (*whom he may or may not have known about*), all born at Bury St Edmunds, were described as 'inmates' at Bury St Edmunds Union Workhouse and Infirmary. The postal address of the workhouse is "*36 Mill Road, Bury St Edmunds*", which is the same address that Fred gave to the Canadian Pioneers for his parents. It would appear that Fred was boarded out to the Simmons family, well away from Bury St Edmunds, where he was born and was brought up in Hailsham until the time that he was sent away '*to help an expanding Empire*'!

༄༄༄༄༄༄༄༄༄

Part Two – The Great War: 1914-18

Atkins, Ernest W.

Rank	Regiment	Age at Death
Lance Sergeant	Royal Sussex	23yrs

Ernest William Atkins was born at Hailsham in February 1893, the son of Arthur and Eliza Atkins and was baptised that year at St Mary's Church. In 1901, he is 8 years old, with two sisters and a brother and living with his parents at 46 High Street, Hailsham. By 1911, at age 18 years, he was boarding with John and Barbara Grayling, (*grandparents?*) at 4 Cobden Place, Hailsham. He was then employed as a School Teacher Assistant at the Council School and was both a keen cricketer and footballer.

On 5 September 1914, he enlisted in Eastbourne into the Royal Sussex Regiment and was recorded as being 5ft 6ins tall with light brown hair and no distinguishing marks.

He served as a Private in the 11th Battalion, 39th Division (*Service No: SD/274*). He was promoted to Lance Corporal in September 1914, full Corporal in April 1916 and Lance-Sergeant on 10 August 1916. In 1914, St Mary's parish magazine reported: -"*Amongst the past and present assistants of the Hailsham Boys School with the Colours are the above (Lieutenant Marillier) .... and Pte E.W.Atkins*". In March 1916, he sent a postcard to Hailsham School letting them know that he was now in France. However, on13 October 1916, the School log books record that he was reported missing and: "*The news has caused quite a gloom amongst the teachers and scholars.*"

Unfortunately, he was already dead when the news was given out as he had been killed in action on 3 September 1916, in the fighting on the Ancre (Hamel) one of the Battles of the Somme, aged 23 years. His death is commemorated on the Thiepval Memorial on the Somme, the largest British war memorial, which contains the names of nearly 73,400 British and South African men who have no known grave and who fell between July 1916 and March 1918 (*Memorial Pier & Face 7C*).

His death is also commemorated on his parent's grave in Hailsham Cemetery (*Grave space: 1002*). Having been both educated and employed at Hailsham Boys School, the name and rank of "*Sergeant E.W. Atkins*" appear on the School Memorial board as well as the Memorial board in St Mary's Church, Hailsham and on the 'Roll of Honour' printed in the parish magazine .

ഝഝഝഝഝഝഝഝഝ

Part Two – The Great War: 1914-18

Barber, Robert W.

Rank	Regiment	Age at Death
Private Private	(1) Royal Sussex (2) Queens (Royal West Surrey)	25yrs

Robert William Barber was born at Eastbourne in 1894, the only child of Frederick and Jane Barber. The family moved to Hailsham and Robert was educated in the town. In 1901, the family were living at Harebeating, Hailsham although Robert's name did not appear on the census return. In 1911, the family were still at Harebeating and Robert, aged 17 years, was described as a kitchen/gardener (domestic). He was in fact working as a groom and gardener to Miss Woodhams, who lived at "Waldernheath", Amberstone in Hailsham. He was a member of the Hailsham Brotherhood and of the Hailsham Agency of the Equitable Friendly Society.

In January 1916, Robert volunteered for Service and enlisted at Eastbourne as a Private into the Royal Sussex Regiment (*Service No: G/8173*). He later transferred into the Queen's, the Royal West Surrey Regiment, (*Service No: G/24512*) where, still as a Private, he served with the 6th Battalion, 12th Division. He went to France three times in all, the last time was in December 1918. He was once slightly wounded in the face by shrapnel. On 9th October 1918, he was acting as sentry and was shot by a sniper, dying immediately. He was 25 years old.

As well as being on the Hailsham War Memorial, his death is commemorated on the Vis en Artois Memorial in the Pas de Calais in France (*Memorial Ref: Panel 3*). This Memorial bears the names of over 9,000 men who fell in the period from 8 August 1918 to the date of the Armistice in the Advance to Victory in Picardy and Artois, between the Somme and Loos, and who have no known grave. Having been educated in Hailsham, the name and rank of *"Private R.W. Barber"* appears on the Hailsham Boys School Memorial board. He is also commemorated on the Memorial board in St Mary's Church, Hailsham and is shown in the parish magazine 'Roll of Honour' as having served in the Queen's Royal West Surrey Regiment.

۩۩۩۩۩۩۩۩۩۩

Part Two – The Great War: 1914-18

Bergan, Otto F.

Rank	Regiment	Age at Death
Lance Corporal	Royal Fusiliers	22yrs

Otto Frederick Bergan (or **Bergann**) was born at Eastbourne in 1894, the son of Otto and Sophie Bergann. The 1901 census shows Otto, then aged 7 years, living in Eastbourne with his parents and three sisters. Ten years later, Otto then aged 17 years was still living with his parents and just two sisters but had no stated occupation. However, as his parents were then the manager and manageress of the Grand Hotel at Dover in Kent, with a range of staff, Otto was probably helping them out in some capacity.

In the 1911 census, Otto's nationality is given as British. However whilst both of his parents are shown as having been born in Germany, his father gives his nationality as Danish whilst his mother gives hers as German. This must have been extremely awkward for them when the war came and could be the reason why Otto dropped his first name and just called himself Frederick.

At the start of the war, Otto, or rather Frederick as he called himself, enlisted into the Royal Fusiliers (*Service No: 3962*) and served as a Private in the 24th Battalion. He was wounded in action in France and returned to England to convalesce. He subsequently died of his wounds on 2nd September 1916 and was buried in Exeter Cemetery. His war service earned him the Victory Medal, the British Medal and also the 1915 Star.

His name appears on the Memorial board placed in St Mary's Church although it had not appeared in the 'Roll of Honour' printed earlier in the parish Magazine. He did not go to school in Hailsham and so his name does not appear on the Boys School Memorial board.

רוֹ רוֹ רוֹ רוֹ רוֹ רוֹ רוֹ רוֹ רוֹ רוֹ

Boniface, George

Rank	Regiment	Age at Death
Private	Royal Sussex	24yrs

George Boniface was, according to military records, born at Eastbourne in 1894. Census records show that there are several George Boniface's born in Eastbourne around the same time and it has not yet been possible to identify this particular one's earlier years or his parents even though he appears to have been brought up in Hailsham. The 1911 census shows that there was a George Boniface, born at Eastbourne, who is boarding with George and Elizabeth Boniface at 49 Station Road, Hailsham. This George is described as being a warehouseman in the grocery trade. This might be the right 'George Boniface' but the the age is different and there is no proof that this person was the one who went to school in Hailsham. 'Our' George Boniface not only went to School at Hailsham Boys School but also played football for the Hailsham Second XI in 1906/07 as shown here.

At the start of the war, George enlisted at Eastbourne into the Royal Sussex Regiment (*Service No: G/16483*) where he served as a Private in the 7th Battalion, 12th Regiment. He was killed in action on 5th April 1918 near Senlis Mill on the Somme. This action relates to the period of crisis in March and April 1918 when the Allied Fifth Army was driven back by overwhelming numbers across the former Somme battlefields, and the months that followed before the Advance to Victory, which began on 8 August 1918.

His death is commemorated on the Poziers Memorial, which commemorates over 14,000 casualties of the United Kingdom and 300 of the South African Forces who have no known grave and who died on the Somme from 21 March to 7 August 1918 (*Memorial Ref: Panel 47*). His war service earned him both the Victory Medal and the British Medal.

The name and rank of "*Private G. Boniface*" appears on the Hailsham Boys School Memorial board and so he must have gone to school in Hailsham. His name is on the Memorial board in St Mary's Church and he is also shown in the 'Roll of Honour' printed earlier in the parish magazine, which states that he was in the 7th Royal Fusiliers but this now is believed to be a mistake. His death is also commemorated on the Memorial board in St Mary's Church, Hailsham as well as that in Christchurch Parish Church, Hampshire. His name also appears on the Eastbourne war Memorial.

ഝഝഝഝഝഝഝഝഝഝ

Part Two – The Great War: 1914-18

Boniface, Louis H.

Rank	Regiment	Age at Death
Private	Suffolk	34yrs

Louis Howard Boniface was born at Hailsham in 1883, the son of Samuel and Mary Boniface. He was later baptised in St Mary's Church in 1894 at the same time as his brother, Martin. In 1891, Louis aged 8 years was living with his parents, Samuel (a hemp spinner) and Mary Boniface, three brothers and one sister in their house in Stoney Lane, Hailsham. One of his brothers was Martin Boniface who was later to die of his wounds a month before Louis himself was killed. Ten years later, the family had moved to 11 South Road, Hailsham and Louis, aged 18 years, shows his occupation as being a bricklayer's labourer. In 1911, not long before the War started, Louis Boniface, then aged 28 years, had left home and was lodging in the home of a widow and her foster family at Hawks Town, Hailsham. He gives his occupation as being a general porter at the East Sussex County Asylum (*Hellingly Hospital*).

He enlisted at the Eastbourne Recruiting Office into the Suffolk Regiment (*Service No: 32249*) and served as a Private. He was transferred into the Suffolk Regiment 2nd Battalion, 3rd Division still as a Private (*Service No: 40909*). He served in France and Flanders and was killed in action on 9th May 1917. He is buried in Feuchy Chapel British Cemetery, Wancourt in the Pas de Calais, France that, at the time of the Armistice, only contained 249 graves (*Grave Ref: I.E.10*). The action in which Louis lost his life centred on the town of Wancourt which was captured in April 1917 after very heavy fighting, lost again in March 1918, and only retaken by the Canadian Corps the following August. His war service earned him both the Victory Medal and the British Medal.

Being a former pupil, his death is commemorated on the Hailsham Boys School Memorial board where he appears as "*Private L.H. Boniface*". His name also appears on the Memorial board in St Mary's Church and also in the parish magazine 'Roll of Honour' which describes him as being a Private in the 2nd Suffolks.

ひひひひひひひひひひ

Part Two – The Great War: 1914-18

Boniface, Martin J.

Rank	Regiment	Age at Death
Private	Royal Sussex	29yrs

Martin John Boniface was born at Hailsham in 1888, the son of Samuel and Mary Boniface. He was later baptised in St Mary's Church in May 1894 along with his brother, Louis. In 1891, aged 3 years old, he was with his parents, Samuel (a hemp spinner) and Mary Boniface, three brothers and one sister in their house in Stoney Lane, Hailsham. One of his brothers was Louis Boniface who was killed in Action just one month after Martin was later to die. In 1901, Martin is aged 12 years and the family had moved to 11 South Road, Hailsham. Ten years later, Martin is aged 22 years and living with his parents and just one brother at 11 South Road, Hailsham. His occupation is described as Bottle Washer/Cellarman, working at the Hailsham Mineral Water Works, a business run by George Guy at 3, North Street, Hailsham.

Martin was already married by the start of the War. He and his wife, Mrs M.A. Boniface, were living at 23 North Street, Hailsham and Martin is described as being the local postman. He enlisted at Herstmonceux into the Royal Sussex Regiment (*Service No: SD/576*) and served as a Private in the 7th Battalion, 12th Division. He was wounded in action and died of his wounds on 27th April 1917, aged 29 years. He is buried in Duisans British Cemetery, Etrun in the Pas de Calais, France (*Grave Ref: II.M.6.*).

Commonwealth forces occupied the area around Duisans from March 1916 but it was not until February 1917 that the site of this cemetery was selected for the 8th Casualty Clearing Station. The first burials took place in March and from the beginning of April the cemetery grew very quickly. Most of the graves relate to the Battles of Arras in 1917 and the trench warfare that followed.

As well as being commemorated on the Hailsham War memorial, Martin Boniface is also commemorated on the Eastbourne War Memorial. Having been educated at Hailsham Boys School, he appears as *"Private M.J. Boniface"* on the Memorial board at the School. His name also appears on the Memorial board in St Mary's Church, Hailsham as well as being in the 'Roll of Honour' printed in the parish magazine, which shows him as having served in the Royal Sussex Regiment.

വവവവവവവവവവ

Part Two – The Great War: 1914-18

Brook, James T.

Rank	Regiment	Age at Death
Private	(1) Royal Army Service Corps	
Private	(2) Royal Welsh Fusiliers	40yrs

James Thomas Brook was born at Hailsham in 1878, the son of John and Susan Brook. In 1891, the family were living at Proclamation House (*now demolished*) in High Street, Hailsham. James was a scholar aged 13 years old, living with his parents, John Brook, a greengrocer, and his wife Susan, together with four younger brothers and four sisters. He married Ellen Fuller around 1899 and in 1901, James was aged 23 years and described as being a 'whitesmith' (*a maker of tin utensils, especially for dairies*) and a gas fitter. He and his wife Ellen were then living at 2, Windsor Road, Hailsham with their 11-month old child, Thomas. Their second child, John (Jack) was born in 1902. They subsequently moved to "The Old Vicarage" in Market
Street, Hailsham where they were living at the start of the war. The photo shown here is of James Brook, his wife Ellen and their two sons, Thomas and Jack. It was taken outside "The Old Vicarage" just before he left home to join up. According to the Sussex Express, James was working then for the ironmongery business of A. F. Smith Ltd, in the High Street, Hailsham.

James enlisted at Chichester initially into the Royal Army Service Corps (*Service No: 180356*) where he served as a Private. He subsequently transferred to the Royal Welsh Fusiliers also as a Private (*Service No: 60572*) where he served in the 17th Battalion. He was in active service in France and Flanders. He was killed in action on 31st July 1917 aged 40 years. This action was at the start of the Third Battle of Ypres, a terrible battle, which, today, is commonly simply referred to as 'Passchendaele'. He has no known grave and his death is commemorated on the Menin Gate Memorial at Ypres in Belgium (*Memorial Ref: Panel 22*).

Having been educated at Hailsham, his name appears on the Hailsham Boys School 'Roll of Honour' as "*Private J.T. Brooks*". It also appears as '*Brooks*' in the 'Roll of Honour' published in St Mary's parish magazine where his Regiment is shown as the Royal Army Service Corps. However, on both the Hailsham war Memorial and also St Mary's Church Roll of Honour', his surname was shown correctly as '*Brook*'.

Butler, Frederick

Rank	Regiment	Age at Death
Able Seaman	HMS. "Good Hope"	34yrs

Frederick Butler was born at Hailsham between July and September 1880, the son of Thomas and Charlotte Butler. In 1891, Frederick aged 10 years is living with his widowed grandmother, Sarah Slaughter, in Carriers Path, Hailsham and there is no trace of his parents. He does not appear in the 1901 census but he subsequently married and in 1911, Frederick Butler, aged 31 years, is living at 2 Coast Guard Cottages, Eastbourne with his wife Lily Butler. They moved sometime later and were living at 2, Bay Cottage, Hailsham Road, Polegate at the time that he joined up. He gives his occupation as a Caretaker working at the General Post Office.

He enlisted into the Royal Navy (*Service No: 198254*) and rose to become an Able Seaman on HMS "*Good Hope*" (*Shown here*). This ship was a 14,100-ton *Drake*-class armoured cruiser of the British Royal Navy, which joined the 6th Cruiser Squadron at the start of the War and, for the next few weeks, was protecting British merchant shipping mainly in the South Atlantic.

On 22 October 1914, the ship then embarked on the search for the German East Asiatic Squadron, leaving Stanley for the west coast of South America via Cape Horn. HMS "*Good Hope*" was the flagship of Admiral Cradock's squadron. At 2000hrs on 1 November 1914, in the Battle of Coronel off the Chilean coast, the combined shelling by the German armoured cruisers *Scharnhorst* and *Gneisenau* under Admiral Graf Maximilian von Spee resulted in a devastating explosion in "Good Hope's" magazine, which tore the ship apart. The entire complement of 900 hands were lost.

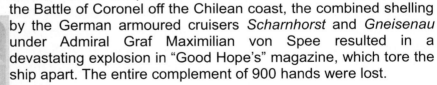

His death is commemorated on the Portsmouth Naval Memorial (*illustrated here*). Having been educated at Hailsham, the name and rank of "*Seaman F. Butler*" appears on the Hailsham Boys School Memorial board. His name also appears on the Memorial board in St Mary's Church, Hailsham and in the 'Roll of Honour' printed earlier in the parish magazine where he is described as *Seaman F. Butler*'.

טטטטטטטטטט

Butler, Richard C.

Rank	Regiment	Age at Death
Sapper	Royal Engineers	38yrs

Richard Charles Butler was born at Hailsham in February 1880, the eldest son of Richard Butler, a builder & wheelwright, and his wife Matilda. In 1891, the family were living in Bellbanks with Richard now shown as aged 11 years, his parents, one younger brother and two sisters. By 1911, the family's address was Buttsfield House, 3 Bellbanks Road, Hailsham. Richard, now aged 31 years, was still living at home with his parents, his brother and just one sister. Richard was assisting in his father's business, which was described as being Builders, Wheelwrights, Undertakers and Timber Merchants.

Richard, at age 36 years and single, enlisted on 20 March 1916 into the Royal Engineers where he served as a sapper (*Service No: 154397*). He gave his trade as being a professional steam sawyer. He was declared medically fit for service, his height was given as 5ft 9¾ins and he had no distinguishing marks. Almost six months later, on 2 October 1916, he was invalided out and discharged as being medically unfit for further war service under *"para 392 XVI King's Regulations."* During that short period, he had developed tuberculosis, which was not the direct result of military service but was aggravated by it. After a further period of sick leave, he was discharged from Grosvenor Sanatorium, Kent on 27th February 1917 and returned home. He subsequently died of his illness at the family home in Bellbanks Road, Hailsham on 23 June 1918, aged 38 years. He is buried in the grave later used by his parents in Hailsham Cemetery (*Grave space 1365*).

Having been brought up and educated in Hailsham, the name and rank of "*Sapper R.C. Butler*" appears on the Hailsham Boys School Memorial board. His name also appears on the Memorial board in St Mary's Church, Hailsham and in the 'Roll of Honour' printed earlier in the parish magazine.

֎֎֎֎֎֎֎֎֎֎֎

Part Two – The Great War: 1914-18

Carter, Nelson V., VC

Rank	Regiment	Age at Death
Coy. Sergeant Major	Royal Sussex	28yrs

Nelson Victor Carter was born at Eastbourne in April 1887, the son of Richard and Harriett Carter. In 1891, the family with Nelson aged 4 years, three brothers and one sister were living at 3 Hydridge Terrace, Latimer Road, Eastbourne. By 1901, the family had moved to Harebeating in Hailsham and Nelson, aged 13, was living there with two brothers and two sisters all children of Richard and Harriett. Nelson was then going to school at Hailsham Boys School. In 1911, Nelson aged 23, had left home and was boarding at 25/27 Upperton Road, Eastbourne and was shown as being employed as a groom.

He married Cathleen Camfield from Rotherfield on 17th October 1911 and they set up home at 33 Greys Road, Eastbourne where they had a daughter, Jesse. At the outbreak of war, he enlisted into the Royal Sussex Regiment in the 11th Battalion, 39th Division (*Service No: SD/4*). He was promoted rapidly, transferred to the 12th Battalion and rose to become Company Sergeant Major. He was killed in the action referred to as the Battle of Boar's Head on the Rue de Bois on 30th June 1916 aged 28 years. This was the same battle in which two of his Hailsham compatriots, David Parsons (1) and Claude Toye also lost their lives. For his actions that day, he was awarded a posthumous Victoria Cross, the highest award in the Commonwealth for Valour and Bravery. His citation read: -

"For most conspicuous bravery. During an attack, he was in command of the fourth wave of the assault. Under intense shell and machine gun fire, he penetrated with a few men into the enemy's second line and inflicted casualties with bombs. When forced to retire to the enemy's first line, he captured a machine gun and shot the gunner with a revolver. Finally after carrying several wounded men to safety, he was himself mortally wounded and died in a few minutes. His conduct throughout the day was magnificent." (NB– A fuller account of this is set out on pages 150 to 153.)

He was buried in the Royal Irish Rifles graveyard at Lavenite, Pas de Calais, in France (*Grave Ref:VI.C.17.*) As well as being commemorated on the Hailsham War Memorial, his name also appears on the Eastbourne Roll of Honour in the Town Hall. Having been brought up and educated at Hailsham, he is commemorated on the Memorial boards in St Mary's Church as well as the Hailsham Council Boys School.

שששששששששש

Part Two – The Great War: 1914-18

Charles, William

Rank	Regiment	Age at Death
Gunner	Royal Field Artillery	40yrs

William Edward Charles was born at Broadwater, Worthing around 1876, the son of Jonathan and Emily Charles. In 1891, he was living at 118 Station Road, East Preston, Brighton. The census then shows him as being aged 15 years old, and his occupation is given as a Page Boy, living with his two brothers and one sister and his parents Jonathan Charles (General Labourer) and Emily (Charwoman). By 1901, he was aged 25 years, had left home and got married. He was living in Worthing with his wife, Louisa Caroline Elizabeth Charles, and working as a market gardener. By 1911, they had moved and both were working as servants, living in at the home of Edmund Strickland, the corn merchant who lived at Summerfields in Western Road, Hailsham. William gave his age as 36 years old and was employed as butler (domestic) to Edmund Strickland whilst his wife, Louisa, is shown as cook/domestic in the same household. He always took a keen interest in the work of Hailsham Parish Church and was a prominent member of the local branch of the Church of England Men's Society. He was also a member of the Hailsham Cricket Club.

At the outbreak of the war, William joined the Hailsham Section of the Ammunition Column of the Royal Field Artillery (Territorial Force) and acted as servant to Captain Gordon Strickland as well as serving as a gunner (*Service No: Gunner 651*). Whilst in training at Slough, where his Regiment was based, he contracted a cold and septic pneumonia set in. He died at the Military Hospital in Southall, Middlesex on 16 December 1914 aged 40 years. His body was brought back to Hailsham and he was accorded full military honours at his funeral. The coffin was covered with the Union Jack flag and the Hailsham Town Prize Band played during the procession. After the service, the firing party fired a three gun salute and the "Last Post" was sounded by the buglers. He was described as *"well known and much respected in Hailsham"*. He is buried in the Hailsham Cemetery (*Grave Space 1202*).

His death is commemorated on the Memorial in St Mary's Church, Hailsham and his name appears in the 'Roll of Honour' printed in the parish magazine where he is shown as '*Gunner, Royal Field Artillery*'.

෴෴෴෴෴෴෴෴෴෴෴

Colarossi, Gilbert

Rank	Regiment	Age at Death
Private	Royal Sussex	19yrs

Gilbert Colarossi was born in Kensington, Middlesex around 1898. His father was Mr F. Albert Colarossi, a married man of Feltham in Middlesex and his mother was Blanche Mary Beet, a married woman, also from Middlesex. Divorce proceedings soon followed and in 1901, Gilbert was living at 37 High Street, Hailsham, aged 3 years old, born in London, along with others and shown as being a 'straggler' (*'nurse child' crossed out*) to Kate Waymark. In 1911, Gilbert, now aged 13 years, is shown as being a 'nurse child' at school, still living with Kate Waymark at 37 High Street, Hailsham.

He was working as a clerk, still living at 37 High Street, when he enlisted on 12th September 1914 at the Herstmonceux recruiting office into the Royal Sussex Regiment. He was actually under age being only 16 years old at the time, but he stated that he had been born in January 1895. This was accepted and he served as a Private (*Service No: SD/581*) in the 11th Battalion, 39th Division. He served in France and was wounded in action. He received gun shot wounds in his back and abdomen during the Battle of Boars Head at Richebourg on 30th June 1916 and returned to England to convalesce. Due to the severity of his wounds, he was posted to the 3rd Battalion of the Royal

Sussex Regiment, which were serving at Newhaven. In November 1917, he was declared physically unfit and discharged from the army. On his discharge papers, as his next-of-kin, Gilbert gives his grandmother, Agnes Dicks, 10 Somerleyton Road, Brixton. Also, but (*crossed out*) he gives his father, Albert Colarossi, c/o Dante, Danesbury Road, Feltham, Middlesex. Gilbert tragically died of his wounds at the Soldiers & Sailors Home, Upperton Road, Eastbourne on 23rd March 1918, aged 19 years. He was buried in Hailsham Cemetery (*Grave space 1704*) in one of the ten WWI graves maintained there by the Commonwealth War Graves Commission.

Having been educated at Hailsham, the name and rank of "*Private G. Colarossi*" appears on the Hailsham Boys School Memorial board. He also appears on the Memorial board in St. Mary's Church, Hailsham as well as in the 'Roll of Honour' printed earlier in the parish magazine.

PS. Gilbert's uncle, Angelo, was the model for the statue of Eros in Picadilly Circus.

Part Two – The Great War: 1914-18

Colbran, Charles

Rank	Regiment	Age at Death
Sapper	Royal Engineers	32yrs

Charles Jesse Colbran, (usually known as Jesse) was born in January 1887, the son of William and Sarah Colbran. In 1891, Charles is four years old and his birthplace is given as Upper Dicker. He was living with his parents and four siblings at New Bridge near Magham Down in Hailsham. Ten years later, the family had moved to Rookery Cottages, in Hailsham, one brother had left home and he had another two younger siblings. Charles was then aged 14 years, his birthplace is now shown as Arlington and he was employed as a '*string planer*' at the Rope Factory. By 1911, Charles had chosen his career as a carpenter and was living at home with his parents, a younger brother and sister at 29 Garfield Road, Hailsham.

On 27 October 1915, Charles married Hilda Louise Hudson at East Hoathly Parish Church. The new couple went to live at 5 Folkington Cottages, near Polegate and their daughter, Sylvia, was born in August 1916.

Just over a month after his wedding, Charles was called up and enlisted at Eastbourne. He was a short man, only 5ft 1ins in height with no distinguishing marks and joined the Royal Engineers as a Private (*Service No: 217401*), this time giving his birthplace as Upper Dicker. On his mobilisation in December 1916, Charles was shown as a proficient carpenter and given the rank of Sapper. In November 1917, he was transferred to the West Yorkshire Regiment but was apparently re-transferred back to the Royal Engineers on the same day, this time with the 504th Field Company. He survived the war but the Regiment had to stay behind in Germany on burial duties. Charles was involved with making coffins and temporary grave markers. On 29 April 1919, he contracted diphtheria. After he ceased to be infectious, he became steadily ill and died on 30 May 1919.

His death was officially diagnosed as tuberculosis, aggravated by diphtheria contracted during service with the British Army of the Rhine. However, a friend later told his wife that he had slipped with a blunt chisel, the cut became infected and that he had actually died from septicaemia. He was buried in Cologne Southern Cemetery in Germany (*Grave Ref: IV.B.2.*). The photo shows his original grave marker, since replaced by one from the Commonwealth War Graves Commission. His widow received an army pension of 26/8d per week plus 10/- for their one child. His war service posthumously earned him both the British War Medal and the Victory Medal.

🙪🙪🙪🙪🙪🙪🙪🙪🙪🙪

Cousens, Alfred S.

Rank	Regiment	Age at Death
Driver	Royal Field Artillery	23yrs

Alfred Stanley Cousens was born at Little Common, near Bexhill in 1895, the son of Henry and Caroline Cousens. In 1911, Alfred, then aged 16 years, was living with his parents and five brothers at 44 South Road, Hailsham. He was an apprentice, boot trade, working at a boot repair shop. Shortly after this, he went to work in the matting department of Burfields, the Rope and Twine factory in South Road, Hailsham and was still working there when he was conscripted.

Alfred enlisted on 5th August 1912 into the Royal Field Artillery and served at home. At the start of the war, he went abroad to India with the 1/5th Sussex Battery, 2nd Home Counties Brigade as a Driver (*Service No: Driver 611*). He was admitted to Ambala

British Military Hospital in the Punjab suffering from tuberculosis. His father later stated that this was caused by injuries received on 10th June 1915 but no details are given. He was discharged as no longer fit for war service on 9th October 1915 and repatriated to England. He was awarded a pension of 20 shillings per week from 1st March 1916. He died on 6th May 1918 whilst at the South Eastern Hospital, Avonley Road at New Cross. His parents were then living at 21 New Road, Hellingly and they had his body brought back to Hailsham. He is buried in Hailsham Cemetery, in one of the ten WWI graves maintained there by the Commonwealth War Graves Commission (*Grave space 1578*).

In June 1918, the Hailsham Parish Magazine carried the following comments: *Mrs Cousens of South Road asks us to convey her best thanks to all who kindly sympathised with her in her bereavement. Her son lost his life indirectly to an accident incurred on active service.*

Having been educated at Hailsham, he is commemorated on the Roll of Honour at Hailsham Boys School. He is also commemorated on the Memorial board in St Mary's Church, Hailsham and in the 'Roll of Honour' printed earlier in the parish magazine. His name also appears in the 'Roll of Honour' written in Burfields day book under the heading "*The Factory Recorder*". As well as the British War Medal, he was also awarded the Territorial Force War Medal.

꠵꠵꠵꠵꠵꠵꠵꠵꠵꠵

Part Two – The Great War: 1914-18

Cox, Herbert

Rank	Regiment	Age at Death
Private	Sherwood Foresters (Notts & Derby)	36yrs

Herbert Cox was always known throughout his life as either Bert or Bertie. He was born in Ashill, near Swaffham in Norfolk in 1882, the son of William and Susannah Cox. The family subsequently moved to Hailsham where Bert was brought up and educated. In 1891, the family were living in Hempstead Lane, Hailsham and Bertie was aged 9 years old. In 1901, he is shown as being 19 years old, single and living with his parents and an elder brother at "Hencoop Cottage", Market Street, Hailsham. His occupation was given as a general labourer. In 1911, Bertie was 29 years old and employed as a Road Labourer, working for the County Council whilst his father was a carter on a farm.

He enlisted at Eastbourne into the Notts & Derby Regiment, the Sherwood Foresters and served as a Private (*Service No: 306917*) in the 1st Battalion, 23rd Division. He was killed in action during the March Retreat on 26 March 1918. This was the period of crisis in March and April 1918 and the months that followed when the Allied Fifth Army was driven back across the former Somme battlefields before the Advance to Victory, which began on 8 August 1918.

His death is commemorated on the Poziers memorial in France, which commemorates over 14,000 casualties of the United Kingdom and 300 of the South African Forces who have no known grave and who died on the Somme from 21 March to 7 August 1918 (*Memorial Ref: Panel 54*).

Having been brought up and educated in Hailsham, the name and rank of "*Private H. Cox*" appears on the Hailsham Boys School Memorial board. His name also appears on the Memorial board in St Mary's Church, Hailsham although it did not appear in the 'Roll of Honour' printed earlier in the parish magazine.

۩ ۩ ۩ ۩ ۩ ۩ ۩ ۩ ۩ ۩

Part Two – The Great War: 1914-18

Davis, Thomas

Rank	Regiment	Age at Death
Private Private	(1) Royal Sussex (2) Machine Gun Corps	27yrs

Thomas Davis was born at Battle in late 1889, the son of Thomas and Jane Davis. In 1891, Thomas was living at 26a Mount Street, Battle, aged 1 year old with one brother and one sister, all of whom are shown as the children of Thomas Davis, a wheelwright/blacksmith, and Jane his wife. By 1901, misfortune had struck, Thomas' mother had died and, around 1899, his father had remarried. The new family then moved to Hailsham and were living in Station Road, where Thomas' father was a coach-builder at the Hailsham Carriage Works. In 1911, Thomas now aged 21 years, is living with his father Thomas and Minnie his wife of 12 years, together with two brothers, at 2 South Road, Hailsham. His occupation is shown as a jobbing carpenter.

Thomas enlisted at Eastbourne on 8 February 1916, presumably giving a false date of birth as he was under-age, into the Royal Sussex Regiment (*Service No: G/5368*). His service record shows that he was born at Hailsham instead of Battle but this could be

incorrect. He later transferred to the Machine Gun Corps (Infantry) where he served as a Private (*Service No: 30336*) with the 123rd Company. He developed pneumonia on 23 November 1916 and was transferred to a casualty clearing station in France. He died 6 days later on 29 November 1916. This was in the final days of the 'War of Attrition' on the Somme.

Military records and his gravestone show him as being 30 years old but he was actually 27 years old. He is buried in Lijssenthoek Military Cemetery at Poperinge, West-Vlaanderen in Belgium (*Grave Ref: X.C.17*). This is the second largest Commonwealth cemetery in Belgium and contains nearly 10,000 Commonwealth burials of the First World War, 24 being unidentified. There are also war graves of other nationalities, mostly French and German.

Having been educated in Hailsham, the name and rank of "*Private T. Davis*" appears on the Hailsham Boys School Memorial board. He is also commemorated on the Memorial board in St Mary's Church, Hailsham and his name appears in the 'Roll of Honour' printed earlier in the parish magazine where he is shown as a Private in the Machine Gun Corps.

ꙭ ꙭ ꙭ ꙭ ꙭ ꙭ ꙭ ꙭ ꙭ ꙭ

Part Two – The Great War: 1914-18

Deacon, Frederick

Rank	Regiment	Age at Death
Private Lance Corporal	(1) Royal Sussex (2) East Kent (The Buffs)	24yrs

Kit & Fred Deacon. Fred was killed in action, in France, during the 1914-18 War, aged 24.

Frederick Deacon (always known as Fred) was born in Hailsham in April 1894, the son of Stephen and Emily Deacon. In 1901, Fred, aged 6 years old and 'at school' was living with his parents, two sisters and six brothers at Little Mulbrooks in Hailsham. In 1911, Fred now aged 16 years, was still living at home, this time with just three brothers and one sister at Saltmarsh Farm in Hailsham. He is shown as being a farm worker.

He enlisted into the army at Hailsham on 24 February 1913 for a four-year term and joined the 5th Royal Sussex Regiment (*Service No: 1619*). For the first 3½ years, he served at Home before being sent to France on 22 September 1916. Shortly after he arrived, he was transferred into the Buffs, (East Kent Regiment) where he served in the 6th Battalion (*Service No. G/12820*). He was appointed as unpaid Lance Corporal on 20 December 1917 and this rank was substantiated on 14 April 1918. He returned home on leave and married Kate (*Kit*) Phipps, a teacher at Rye Grammar School, at Hailsham on 15 June 1918. They set up home at 8 Waterloo Place in Rye but Fred had to return to France. He took part in the Advance to Victory in Picardy and Artois but was killed in action on 22 September 1918 during one of the battles of the Hindenburg Line. He was aged 24 years. It was just three months after his wedding and only a few weeks away from the end of the war. His widow was sent both the British and Victory Medals for his war service.

His death is recorded on the Vis-en-Artois Memorial in the Pas de Calais area of France, as he has no known grave (*Memorial Ref: Panel 3*). He is also commemorated on his father's gravestone in Hailsham Cemetery (*Grave No: OE*). Having been educated in Hailsham, the name and rank of "*Corporal F. Deacon*" appears on the Hailsham Boys School Memorial board. His name also appears on the Memorial board in St Mary's Church, Hailsham as well as in the 'Roll of Honour' printed earlier in the Parish magazine.

৬৫৬৫৬৫৬৫৬৫৬৫৬৫৬৫৬৫৬৫

Divall, Charles H.

Rank	Regiment	Age at Death
Private Private	(1) Royal Sussex (2) Bedfordshire	25yrs

Charles Henry Divall was born at Hailsham in November 1893, the son of Emma Divall and was baptised in February 1894 at St Mary's Church, Hailsham. In 1901, Charles was living in Hellingly, aged 7 years, along with his brother and sister, all shown as being children of Emma Divall, a widow. In 1911, Charles, now aged 17 years, was living-in at a small school, "Rathgowry", Mount Road, Eastbourne where he was employed as a gardener.

Charles enlisted at Eastbourne on 28th September 1915 and he was described as 5ft 6ins tall. He gave his mother as next of kin, his occupation as a gardener and his address as 12 Battle Road, Hailsham. He joined the Royal Sussex Regiment as a Private (*Service No: G/7942*) but shortly afterwards, transferred to the Bedfordshire Regiment as a Private (*Service No: 23867*) with the 1st Garrison Battalion.

On 26th February 1916, he went with the Regiment to India where he stayed for the next two years. He was admitted to the Station Hospital in Delhi on 28th February 1917 with a fistula and was operated on shortly afterwards. He appears to have stayed in hospital for some time and was diagnosed with tuberculosis. On 17th August 1917, the medical board declared him as unfit for further service. Charles was returned to England to convalesce. On 16th March 1918, the Final Medical Board was of the opinion that his disability was *"caused by service during the present war"*. He was awarded a pension of 27/6d per week and discharged from the army.

Tragically, he died of his illness at his home, 12 Battle Road, Hailsham, on 5th January 1919 and is buried in Hailsham Cemetery in one of the ten WWI graves maintained there by the Commonwealth War Graves Commission (*Grave space 802*).

Having been educated at Hailsham, the name and rank of *"Private C.H. Divall"* appears on the Hailsham Boys School Memorial board. His name also appears on the Memorial board in St Mary's Church, Hailsham. Being apparently a member of the Wesleyan congregation, he is also commemorated on the Memorial tablet at the Hailsham Methodist Church.

വവവവവവവവവവവ

Part Two – The Great War: 1914-18

Elphick, Walter

Rank	Regiment	Age at Death
Private	Royal Sussex	27yrs

Walter Elphick was born at Hailsham in 1892, the only son of Caleb and Rhoda Elphick. In 1901, the census return shows his parents living at Downash in Hailsham but Walter himself was not shown for some reason. However, in 1911, he is shown as living with his parents, this time at Vicarage Cottage, Market Street, Hailsham. He was then 19 years old and employed as a general hand for Mr Crowhurst at Messrs Southerden and Crowhurst, wine and spirit merchants in North Street, Hailsham and was still working there when he was called up.

He enlisted on 11th January 1915 at the Hastings Recruiting Office into the Royal Sussex Regiment, where he served as a Private (*Service No: G/6354*) in the 7th Battalion, 12th Division. He went to the Front at the end of March 1915. In April 1916, he received a shrapnel wound under his left arm and was sent back to the Military Hospital in Bristol where he recovered. He returned to the Front but was killed in action near Epehy Wood on 18 September 1918, aged 27 years. He is buried in Epehy Wood Farm Cemetery (*Grave Ref: II.D.12*).

The village of Epehy is in the Somme Department of France and was captured by the Allies at the beginning of April 1917. It was lost in March 1918 after a spirited defence by the Leicester Brigade of the 21st Division and the 2nd Royal Munster Fusiliers. It was retaken on 18 September 1918, by various regiments of the 12th (Eastern) Division and it was during that action that Walter Elphick lost his life.

Having been educated at Hailsham, the name and rank of "*Private W. Elphick*" appears on the Hailsham Boys School Memorial board. His name also appears on the Memorial board in St Mary's Church, Hailsham as well as in the 'Roll of Honour' printed in the parish magazine where he is shown as a Private in the Royal Sussex Regiment.

ഇഇഇഇഇഇഇഇഇഇ

Part Two – The Great War: 1914-18

Firrell, Frank

Rank	Regiment	Age at Death
Lance Corporal	Royal Sussex	26yrs

Frank Jabez Firrell was born in Hailsham in November 1889. In the 1891 census, Frank was living at the family home in Battle Road, Hailsham, aged 1 year old, together with his three elder brothers and two sisters, all of which are shown as the children of Moses Firrell, a (domestic) coachman and Mary his wife. In 1911, Frank, then aged 21 years, was still living with his parents, Moses and Mary Firrell, and just two sisters, at 59 High Street, Hailsham. He was employed as a shop assistant for his father who was now a greengrocer.

Frank enlisted as soon as the war started on 5th September 1914 at the Eastbourne Recruiting Office for a three-year period with the colours into the Royal Sussex Regiment, where he served in the 11th Battalion, 39th Division (*Service No: SD/306*). Within a few months, on 23rd December 1914, he was appointed Lance Corporal, although this was unpaid. He went to the Front on 4 March 1915 and was only appointed as a paid Lance Corporal some fourteen months later on 19th February 1916. He was killed whilst on patrol duty on 3rd June 1916, aged 26 years, near Cambrin, on the Ypres Salient. This action was part of the build up to the Allied Offensive on the Somme.

Lieutenant Cassels wrote the following letter to his parents: - *"He went out in the early morning (after we had repelled a party of the enemy whose intention it was to bomb us) to see what damage we had done to them. An enemy sniper shot him in the head and he died instantly suffering no pain. Since we have been in France, your son had shown himself to be a hard-working and very fearless soldier, always cheery and in the best of spirits. He was very keen on patrol work and his name was twice put in battalion orders for the good work he had done."*

Frank was buried in Cambrin Churchyard Extension, in the Pas de Calais Department of France (*Grave Ref: M.4.*). At one time, the village of Cambrin housed Brigade headquarters but until the end of the First World War, it was only about 800 metres from the front line trenches. This Extension contains just over 1,200 Commonwealth burials of the First World War.

Having been educated at Hailsham, the name and rank of *"Lance Corporal F. Firrell"* appears on the Hailsham Boys School Memorial board. His name also appears on the Memorial board in St Mary's Church as well as in the 'Roll of Honour' printed earlier in the parish magazine.

৸৸৸৸৸৸৸৸৸৸

Part Two – The Great War: 1914-18

Fox, William

Rank	Regiment	Age at Death
Private	The Buffs (East Kent)	22yrs

William Thomas Gordon Fox was born at Cinderford, near Hailsham in 1897, the son of William and Caroline Fox. In 1911, William, then aged 14 years but shown as having been born at Herstmonceux, was living with his parents, three brothers and two sisters at 69 South Road, Hailsham. His occupation is described as 'pulling down yarn' at Burfield's brush mat factory, in South Road, Hailsham where his father also worked. He continued working at Burfields, the Rope and Twine factory in Hailsham and was working there at the start of the war when he was conscripted.

He enlisted at the Eastbourne Recruiting Office into the East Kent Regiment. He served as a Private (*Service No: G/12509*) in the 7th Battalion, 18th Division although, according to Burfield's record book, he appears to have been attached to the Royal Engineers. He was captured and taken prisoner. Tragically he died in captivity in one of the prisoner of war camps in Germany, aged 22 years. His death was given as 10th November 1918, which is the day before the Armstice was signed. Records of prisoners of war in WW I are very difficult to come across. Without knowing the name of the camp and therefore the date when it was reached by the Allies, it is open to conjecture as to whether he was already dead when the camp was reached or whether he died after it was liberated. He is buried in Cologne Southern Cemetery in Germany (*Grave Ref: XII.G.12*).

Cologne was entered by Commonwealth forces on 6 December 1918 and occupied under the terms of the Treaty of Versailles until January 1926. Cologne Southern Cemetery was used during the war for the burial of more than 1,000 Allied prisoners of war, as well as German servicemen. There are now nearly 2,500 First World War servicemen buried or commemorated in the Commonwealth plots at Cologne.

Having been educated in Hailsham, the name and rank of "*Private W. Fox*" appears on the Hailsham Boys School Memorial board. His name also appears on the Memorial board in St Mary's Church, Hailsham although it did not appear in the 'Roll of Honour' printed earlier in the parish magazine. His name is also shown in Burfields 'Roll of Honour' written in their day book under the heading "*The Factory Recorder*" which shows his regiment as being "*Attached R.E.*".

಄ ಄ ಄ ಄ ಄ ಄ ಄ ಄ ಄ ಄

Part Two – The Great War: 1914-18

Funnell, Herbert L.

Rank	Regiment	Age at Death
(?)	(?)	46 yrs

Herbert Leonard Funnell is one whose background and family life have been rather difficult to trace because there were many people with the surname of Funnell living around Hailsham at that time. It finally transpires that he was the son of Cornelius Funnell, a labourer in a corn store, and his wife Charlotte and was born in Hailsham on 30 November 1873. In 1881, he was shown as a scholar, living with his parents and two sisters at 7 Buttsfield, Hailsham. Ten years later, at age 17 years, he is still at home, this time at 9 Devonshire Place, Hailsham. No occupation is shown for him and his name has been entered on the return as Leonard. By 1901, he had left home and was boarding with an older couple, unrelated, at 21 Western Road, Bexhill. He is then aged 28 years old and working as a grocer's assistant.

By the time of the 1911 census, everything had changed in Herbert's life. His father had died and his mother was living with her married daughter. Herbert, on the other hand, had moved out of the area and was working as a railway clerk aged 37 years. He had been married for some ten years and now had four children, one daughter and three sons. His wife's name was Ellen Elizabeth and they were living at 58a Deacon Road, Willesden Green, Middlesex. It is believed that their family apparently increased to eight children.

His military service has not yet been ascertained. However, he probably joined one of the army regiments as he appears to have either been wounded or was discharged and sent home to convalesce. He died after the war had ended at Willesden on 26 May 1920 aged 46 years and was possibly buried in the local cemetery.

His name is not shown in the initial 'Roll of Honour' printed in the parish magazine although it does appear on the Memorial board in St Mary's Church. It does not show on the Memorial board in Hailsham Council Boys School because this was unveiled in 1919. The name of Herbert L. Funnell was one of the eleven names added later to the High Street Memorial.

஫஫஫஫஫஫஫஫஫஫

Part Two – The Great War: 1914-18

Gadd, James G.

Rank	Regiment	Age at Death
Private	Royal Sussex	36yrs

James George Gadd was born in 1879 in Goudhurst, Kent, the son of James, an agricultural worker, and Cecilia Gadd. In 1881, aged 2 years, James is living with his parents and four elder sisters at Pepperingeye Farm, near Battle. In 1891, aged 12 years old, he is a 'visitor' in the home of Oliver and Sarah Firrell and their son James H. Firrell at Broad Oak, Brede. Ten years later, at age 22, he is boarding out at 5 Sexton Cottages, Hailsham and shows his employment as being a labourer/bricklayer. Around 1903, James married Annie Parsons, who came from Hailsham. In 1911, James Gadd, then giving his age as 30 years was employed by Mr F. Langley, the local coal man as a coal porter. In addition, James and Annie, were living at 6 Victoria Road, Hailsham with James' widowed father-in-law, David Parsons and the first two of their eventual three daughters.

James enlisted at London into the Royal Sussex Regiment and served as a Private (*Service No: SD/4213*) in the 13th Battalion, 39th Division. He was killed in action on 30th June 1916 aged 36 years during the Battle of Boar's Head on the Rue de Bois, Pas de Calais, in France. This was the disastrous day when Nelson Carter, David Parsons (1) and Claude Toye were also killed. James' death is commemorated on The Loos Memorial, Pas de Calais, France (*Memorial Ref: Panel 69 to 73*). This Memorial forms the sides and back of Dud Corner Cemetery. It commemorates over 20,000 officers and men who have no known grave and who fell in the area from the River Lys to the old southern boundary of the First Army, east and west of Grenay. The official notification of his death, which was sent to his widow, Annie, very unfortunately started off with "Dear Sir" instead of "Dear Madam". Following his death, his widow, Annie, was awarded a pension of two pounds thirteen shillings a week for herself and her three daughters.

Having been educated at Hailsham, the name and rank of "*Private J.G. Gadd*" appears on the Hailsham Boys School Memorial board. His name also appears in the 'Roll of Honour' printed in the parish magazine as well as the Memorial board in St Mary's Church, Hailsham. His war service earned him both the Victory and also the British War Medals.

ഇ ഇ ഇ ഇ ഇ ഇ ഇ ഇ ഇ ഇ

Part Two – The Great War: 1914-18

Gater, Ernest R.

Rank	Regiment	Age at Death
Private Private	(1) Essex (2) Machine Gun Corps	19yrs

Ernest Roland Gater was born in Eastbourne in 1899. In 1901, he is on the census, aged 2 years, described as a 'nursechild' at 5 Tideswell Road, Eastbourne at the home of William and Frances Carey. By 1911 the family had moved and Ernest, then aged 12 years and at school, was shown as boarding, along with another boarder, at 33 Windsor Road, Hailsham, which was, again, the home of William and Frances Carey.

Ernest enlisted at the Lewes Recruiting Office initially as a Private into the Essex Regiment (*Service No: 2809*). He subsequently transferred to the Machine Gun Corps where he served as a Private (*Service No: 149635*). He was killed in action on 21st September 1918, aged 19 years. The town of Villers-Guislain was occupied by Commonwealth forces from April 1917 until the German counter attacks in the Battle of Cambrai at the end of November 1917. It was lost on 30 November and regained by the Germans on 1 December in spite of the fierce attacks of the Guards Division and tanks. The Germans finally abandoned the village at the end of September 1918, after some heavy fighting and it was during this action that Ernest Gater lost his life.

He was buried in Villiers Hill British Cemetery, Villers-Guislain in France (*Grave Ref: VI.D.27*).

Having been a pupil at Hailsham, the name and rank of "*Private E.R. Gates*", (*mis-spelt*), appears on the Hailsham Boys School Memorial board. His name also appears (*correctly*) on the Memorial board in St Mary's Church, Hailsham as well as in the 'Roll of Honour' printed earlier in the parish magazine (*also mis-spelt as 'Gates*).

ฆฆฆฆฆฆฆฆฆฆ

Part Two – The Great War: 1914-18

Goad, Charles S.

Rank	Regiment	Age at Death
Driver	Royal Horse/Field Artillery	24yrs

Charles Samuel Goad was born in Hailsham in 1894, the son of George and Harriett Goad and was brought up in the town where he was educated at Hailsham Boys School. In 1911, Charles, then aged 17 years, was employed as a carman working for a coal merchant. He was living at the family home, Havelock House, Harebeating, Hailsham, with his parents, three brothers and two sisters. By 1918, his parents had moved from Harebeating and were living at Longleys Cottages, Harebeating Lane, in Hailsham.

Charles enlisted in 1915 at the Hailsham Recruiting Office into the Royal Horse/Field Artillery (Territorial Force) (*Service No: 905599*) and St Mary's parish magazine records that he was on the 'Roll' of Hailsham men going for service in France as a driver. He later served in the Balkans theatre of war, still as a driver. On 15 September 1918, the Allies in Salonika mounted a fierce attack on Bulgarian formations, which were by now largely denuded of German troops who had been taken for service on the Western Front. The Balkans war lasted until mid November 1918. Charles died in Salonika on 2nd October 1918, aged 24 years. He was buried in Kirechkoi-Hortakoi Cemetery, some 15 kilometres north east of Thessaloniki, in Greece (*Grave Ref: 202*).

This cemetery was begun in March 1916, but it remained a very small one until September 1917, when the 60th, 65th and 66th General Hospitals came to the neighbourhood. In June, July and September 1918, other hospitals were brought to the high and healthy country beside the Salonika-Hortakoi road and in September 1918, the influenza epidemic began which raged for three months and filled three-quarters of the cemetery. It could well have been this epidemic that caused the death of Charles Goad.

Having been educated at Hailsham, the name and rank of "Driver C.S. Goad" appears on the Hailsham Boys School Memorial board. His name also appears on the Memorial boards in both Hailsham Methodist Church and also St Mary's Church, with his regiment being shown in both cases as being the Royal Field Artillery.

෴෴෴෴෴෴෴෴෴෴

Green, Ewart Victor

Rank	Regiment	Age at Death
Rifleman	London (Rifle Brigade)	20yrs

Ewart Victor Green was born in Hailsham in 1897, the eldest son of James and Ann Green of Melbourne Villas, Hailsham. James, his father was described on the census as a twine manufacturer but was, in reality, the head of the well-known Hailsham firm of Green Brothers. In 1901, Ewart was aged 3 years old and the family consisting of James and Ann, Ewart and his two elder brothers were still living at Melbourne Villas. By 1911, Ewart was only 13 and still at home with his parents at Melbourne Villas whilst both brothers who were almost 20 years older than him, had already left home.

Ewart enlisted at Eastbourne recruiting office into the London Regiment where he served as a Rifleman (*Service No: 303088*) in the 2/5th Brigade. He was killed in action at Poelcapelle on 30th October 1917, aged 20 years and is commemorated on the Tyne Cot Memorial in Belgium (*Memorial Ref: Panel 150*). The Tyne Cot Memorial is one of four memorials to the missing in Belgian Flanders, which cover the area known as the Ypres Salient. There are nearly 12,000 Commonwealth servicemen of the First World War buried or commemorated in Tyne Cot Cemetery and almost 8,400 of these are unidentified.

In his Parish letter of December 1917, Rev F. Clyde Harvey wrote as follows: -

"Ewart Victor Green was a delicate lad. He joined the London Rifle Brigade and went to the front. His friends urged him to get some other branch of the Army more suited to his health, but he wrote home "Don't talk to me of such. My place is here till the job's done" – so he fell at Poelcapelle facing the foe."

His name appears on the Memorial board in St Mary's Church, Hailsham as well as being in the 'Roll of Honour' printed earlier in the parish magazine. He is also commemorated with an inscription on his parent's grave in Hailsham Cemetery (*Grave space 792A*). After the war, it was his two older brothers, J. Robert Green and Arthur Green, who later offered and subsequently bought 'South View Villa' which was presented to the Council in memory of their younger brother, Ewart and a commemorative plaque (*see photo*) to his memory hangs in the Memorial Institute Club in Western Road, Hailsham.

🀄🀄🀄🀄🀄🀄🀄🀄🀄🀄

Part Two – The Great War: 1914-18

Gunter, John

Rank	Regiment	Age at Death
Private Private	(1) Somerset Light Infantry (2) Machine Gun Corps	25yrs

John Gunter was born at Mark, in Somerset, in 1891, the son of Henry Gunter, a wheelwright, and his wife, Mary. In 1901, he is living at home with his parents, two brothers and a sister. By 1911, John's father had died and his widowed mother was living at Primrose Cottage, Olveston in Gloucestershire. John had moved away and was boarding at a house in Frome, in Somerset, along with two others, all of whom had their occupations shown as 'printer's apprentice'. Some time after 1911, John moved to Hailsham and was presumably working in the town. His name does not appear in any street directory for Hailsham. The logical reason for this is that he was boarding/lodging in the town as many people did at this time. It could also be assumed that he was carrying out his trade of printing.

John enlisted at the Eastbourne Recruiting Office into the Somerset Light Infantry as a Private (*Service No: 20031*). In December 1915, St Mary's Parish magazine mentions that John was one of the Hailsham men serving with the Colours with the Somerset Light Infantry. He subsequently transferred to the Machine Gun Corps (Infantry) and served as a Private (*Service No: 9875*) in the 149th Company. He was killed in action on 13th April 1916 during one of the actions on the Ypres Salient.

He is buried in La Laiterie Military Cemetery in Belgium (*Grave Ref: IV.A.3*). This cemetery was named from a nearby dairy farm. It was begun in November 1914 and used until October 1918 by units holding this sector of the front.

His name is not shown in the original 'Roll of Honour' printed in the parish magazine although it does appear on the Memorial board in St Mary's Church.

ᴎ ᴎ ᴎ ᴎ ᴎ ᴎ ᴎ ᴎ ᴎ ᴎ

Part Two – The Great War: 1914-18

Hall, Jack

Rank	Regiment	Age at Death
Private	Royal Sussex	19yrs

John William Hall (usually known as Jack) was born in Mayfield around 1896. In 1911, Jack, then aged 15 years, is shown as 'foster son' to Agnes Sherlock and was living at Hawks Town, Hailsham. This is the same house in which Louis H. Boniface was also lodging. Jack is shown as working as a 'wheel boy' at a rope and twine manufacturer, probably Green Brothers, as he is not shown in Burfield's 'Roll of Honour'.

He enlisted at the Brighton Recruiting Office into the Royal Sussex Regiment where he served as a Private in the 2nd battalion, 1st Division in the Western Europe campaign as part of the British Expeditionary Force.

The Battle of Loos lasted from 25 September to 18 October 1915. Compared with the small-scale British efforts of spring 1915, this attack of six Divisions was a mighty offensive indeed - so much so that it was referred to at the time as 'The Big Push'. Taking place on ground not of their choosing and before stocks of ammunition and heavy artillery were sufficient, the opening of the battle was noteworthy for the first use of poison gas by the British Army. Despite heavy casualties, there was considerable success on the first day in breaking into the deep enemy positions near Loos and Hulluch. However, the reserves had been held too far from the battle front to be able to exploit the successes and succeeding days bogged down into attritional warfare for minor gains.

Jack was killed in action during the Battle of Loos on 13th October 1915 at Hulluch and is buried in Phalempin Communal Cemetery, Pas de Calais, in France (*Grave Ref: Plot C.4*). Phalempin is a small village about 12 kilometres south of Lille and, in the small cemetery there, are 42 UK and 2 Canadian burials from the 1st World War.

Having been educated at Hailsham, the name and rank of *"Private J. Hall"* appears on the Hailsham Boys School Memorial board. His name also appears on the Memorial board in St Mary's Church, Hailsham as well as the 'Roll of Honour' printed earlier in the parish magazine.

His war service earned him the 1914 Star with clasp as well as the British and Victory Medals.

ריריריריריריריריריר

Part Two – The Great War: 1914-18

Harriott, James

Rank	Regiment	Age at Death
Private	Essex	44yrs

James Harriott (*or **Herriott** as it was sometimes spelt*) was, according to army service records, born at Rodmell in Sussex around 1874. However, the census returns give his birth place as Eastbourne.

In 1901, James Harriott is shown as the nephew of Stephen and Elizabeth Fox, born in Eastbourne, aged 27 years, employed as a mat maker and living at 19 Garfield Road, in Hailsham. In 1911, at age 37 years, James is shown as boarding at 9 Gordon Place, the home of Isabel Fox. His occupation is now given as '*Factory String Walker*' and he again gives his birthplace as being Eastbourne. Later information shows that he was working at Burfields Rope and Twine Factory in South Road, Hailsham.

He was still living and working in Hailsham but it was at Brighton Recruiting Office where he enlisted into the Essex Regiment. He served with this Regiment as a Private (*Service No: 57830*) in the 17th Battalion.

It appears that he was badly wounded in action and returned home to England to convalesce. Tragically, he died of his wounds, possibly at one of the military hospitals, on 29th October 1918. He is buried at Horsham (Hills) Cemetery (*Grave Ref: G.104*).

His name is shown on the Memorial board in St Mary's Church, Hailsham although it is not shown in the 'Roll of Honour' printed earlier in the parish magazine. His name also appears in Burfield's 'Roll of Honour' under the heading "The Factory Recorder". Whilst this does not show his department, or the regiment that he joined, this does show that he died on 29th October 1918. His name, however, is recorded as Herriott instead of Harriott.

ॼॼॼॼॼॼॼॼॼॼ

Part Two – The Great War: 1914-18

Harvey, Richard Ernest

Rank	Regiment	Age at Death
Captain (Adjutant)	Black Watch (Royal Highland)	24yrs

Richard Ernest Harvey was born at Hailsham, along with his twin sister Dorothy, in 1891 to Prebendary Francis Clyde Harvey and his wife, Ellen. His father was the vicar of St Mary's Parish Church in Hailsham and, in the census of that year, Richard was living at The Vicarage, Hailsham, aged 2 months old. The family consisted of his parents, Richard's twin sister, three elder brothers and four other sisters. One of his brothers was Rollo Harvey, who was subsequently killed in action some nine months after Richard was. In 1911, Richard Harvey, then aged 20 years, was living with his parents at Hailsham Vicarage along with three sisters but not his elder brother, Rollo. He is shown as being an undergraduate at Exeter College, Oxford.

Richard gained a commission into the Royal Highland Regiment, the Black Watch and served as a Captain (Adjutant) in the 9th Battalion, 15th Scottish Division. During the Battle of Loos, on 25th September 1915, the Battalion had orders to charge at 6.30am and take two trenches. Whilst Captain Harvey was taking orders from the Colonel to the various companies and passing from one trench to another, he was shot just above the heart. He was taken to the field dressing station where he was declared dead on arrival. He was 24 years old.

Captain Richard Harvey is buried in Fosse 7 Military Cemetery, Mazingarbe in Pas de Calais, France (*Grave Ref: I.B.9*). This cemetery was begun by French troops in May 1915, and carried on by British units from June 1915 to April 1917. It is also named "Quality Street" and it is believed that the cemetery takes its name from the pithead, which stood nearby.

He is shown as Captain & Adjutant, 9th Black Watch in the parish magazine in December 1918 and this also appears on the Memorial board in St Mary's Church, Hailsham.

ΩΩΩΩΩΩΩΩΩΩ

Part Two – The Great War: 1914-18

Harvey, Rollo D'Aubigne

Rank	Regiment	Age at Death
Acting Captain	Royal Sussex	31yrs

Rollo D'Aubigne Harvey was born at Eastbourne, along with his twin brother Clyde, in 1885, the son of Prebendary Francis Clyde Harvey and his wife, Ellen. In 1891, Rollo, then aged 6 years old, was living with his family at The Vicarage, Hailsham. His family consisted of his parents Francis C. Harvey (Vicar of Hailsham) and Ellen his wife, his three brothers and four sisters. One of his brothers was Richard who was subsequently killed in action some nine months before Rollo was himself killed. In 1901, Rollo was a 16 year old boarder at Marlborough College in Wiltshire. For some reason, Rollo does not appear in the 1911 census. However, he was still studying in the ministry, (presumably to follow in his father's footsteps) as he gave studying up when he entered the army.

Rollo joined up soon after the war started and enlisted into the Royal Sussex Regiment. He gained a commission and served with the rank of Lieutenant in the 2nd Battalion, 1st Division. He went to the Front in July 1916 and rose to the rank of Acting Captain. He was killed in action at Ginch on the Somme on 9th September 1916, aged 31 years.

He was buried in Caterpillar Valley Cemetery (*Grave Ref: IX.D.22*). This was the name given by the army to the long valley, which rises eastwards, past "Caterpillar Wood", to the high ground at Guillemont . The ground was captured, after very fierce fighting, in the latter part of July 1916. It was lost in the German advance of March 1918 but recovered by the 38th (Welsh) Division on 28 August 1918. After the Armistice, this cemetery was hugely increased when the graves of more than 5,500 officers and men were brought in from other small cemeteries, and the battlefields of the Somme. The great majority of these soldiers died in the autumn of 1916.

His name appears on the Memorial board in St Mary's Church, Hailsham as well as in the 'Roll of Honour' printed earlier in the parish magazine.

His war service earned him both the British and Victory Medals.

﬚﬚﬚﬚﬚﬚﬚﬚﬚﬚﬚

Part Two – The Great War: 1914-18

Hollebon, Charles

Rank	Regiment	Age at Death
Private	Royal Sussex	20yrs

Charles James Hollebon was born in Hailsham in 1896. He was the third son of Thomas Henry and Harriett Eleanor Hollebon of 12 Garfield Road, Hailsham. Thomas Hollebon died in May 1907, when Charles was just over 10 years old and his mother was left to bring up the family. In 1911, Charles, then aged 15 years, was employed as a 'newsboy' with W. H. Smith & Son in their shop situated on the south side of Hailsham railway station. He was living at 31 Garfield Road, Hailsham with his widowed mother, Harriett, three brothers and one sister. In 1914, before he enlisted, he was in charge of Messrs W.H. Smith & Sons sub-stall at Horeham (*sic*) Railway Station.

He enlisted just before Christmas 1914 at the Eastbourne Recruiting Office into the Royal Sussex Regiment and served as a Private in the 2nd Battalion (*Service No: G/4688*). Following basic training, he went to France to the Front in March 1915 and was transferred to the 3rd battalion. He took part in the disastrous '*historic charge*' when the British Troops went '*over the top*' at Aubers Ridge, near Richebourg L'Avoue in France on 9th May 1915 and over 11,000 men were killed (*See page 110 for further details*). Initially he was reported as 'missing' and a chum (*Charlie Spiers*) wrote saying that he had seen 'Charlie' after the charge, limping along, wounded and apparently making for a place of safety. However, it was eventually confirmed that he had been killed in action that day aged 20 years old. This was the same action in which his fellow Hailsham comrades George Smith, John Tingley and Edgar Rigelsford were also killed. Charles had been in France less than two months when he died.

He is commemorated on The Le Touret Memorial, in Richebourg-l'Avoue, France which is one of those erected to record the names of the officers and men who fell in the Great War and whose graves are not known (*Memorial Ref: Panel 20 & 21*).

Having been brought up and educated at Hailsham, the name and rank of "*Private C. Hollebone*" (*surname slightly mis-spelt*) appears on the Hailsham Boys School Memorial board. His name also appears on the Memorial board in St Mary's Church, Hailsham as well as in the 'Roll of Honour' printed earlier in the parish magazine. His war service earned him the 1915 Star and the British and Victory Medals.

๚๚๚๚๚๚๚๚๚๚

Part Two – The Great War: 1914-18

Hollebone, Charles

Rank	Regiment	Age at Death
Private Private	(1) Lincolnshire (2) Royal Defence Corps	21yrs

Charles Hollibone (*Sometimes spelt as Hollebone*) was born in Hailsham in 1899, the son of Charles and Caroline Alice Hollibone. In 1911, Charles, then aged 12 years, was at school and living with his parents at a house in Battle Road, Hailsham together with his one brother and two sisters. His brother, Henry Walter was also killed during the war after his ship was mined.

Charles was living at "Woodlands", Harebeating (Battle Road) in Hailsham and was aged 18 years and 12 days when he enlisted in December 1916 at the Chichester Recruiting Office. He joined the Lincolnshire Regiment where he served as a Private in the 26th Battalion (*Service No: TR/196023*). On enlistment, he gave his occupation as being a gardener and his father, Charles, as being his next-of-kin.

He was wounded in action and records show that he had received a gun-shot wound in the chest. Because of this, he was transferred to the Royal Defence Corps where he served as a Private (*Service No: 93337*) in the 200th Protection Company. The Royal Defence Corps was formed in August 1917 from the Home Service Garrison Battalions of 18 Regiments. It was made up of soldiers who were beyond the age set for combatant service, or those who were not fit for duty overseas, sometimes as the result of wounds received on active service. The Corps was similar in some ways to the Home Guard of the Second World War. Its job was to guard railways, tunnels, roads and ports, thus relieving other troops for front line service. Charles was discharged on 21st February 1919 and came home.

On his return to his parent's home at "Woodlands", Battle Road in Hailsham, he was hospitalised at the Princess Alice Memorial Hospital in Eastbourne. He remained there as a patient for the next ten months before he finally died of his war wounds on 19th October 1920 aged 21 years. Described as a 'discharged soldier', he was buried in Hailsham Cemetery in one of the ten WWI graves maintained by the Commonwealth War Graves Commission (*Grave space 1237*).

His late death means that his name does not appear on the Memorial board at Hailsham Boys School although it does appear on the Memorial board in St Mary's Church, Hailsham.

வ வ வ வ வ வ வ வ வ வ

Hollibone, Henry W.

Rank	Regiment	Age at Death
Bombardier Seaman	(1) Royal Horse Artillery (2) HMS "Laforey"	23yrs

Henry Walter Hollibone was born in Hailsham on 26 December 1893, the son of Charles and Caroline Alice Hollibone. In 1911, Henry then aged 17 years, was described as a 'puller down' in the mat factory of Mssrs. Burfield & Son. He was living with his parents at "Woodlands", Battle Road, Hailsham with his two sisters and one brother Charles who also lost his life in the war.

Henry enlisted at the Drill Hall in Hailsham on 27th November 1911 into the Royal Horse Artillery where he served as a gunner (*Service No: 206*). In August 1914, he went to France and on 1st May 1915, was promoted to Bombardier. He was eventually discharged with an exemplary character on 24th March 1916 and transferred to Army Reserve. Whilst in the Army, he married Frances and they set up home at "Park View", Coombe, near Sandwich in Kent. On his discharge, he was recorded as 5ft 9ins high, dark complexion, brown eyes, dark brown hair and several tattoos. The one on his right forearm between "*Clasp hands and heart*" and "*Winged horse*" was "*Frances true love*". He gave his occupation as a chauffeur.

He apparently did not settle as he subsequently enlisted into the Royal Navy where he served as an Ordinary Seaman (*Service No: J/57195*) on HMS "Laforey" (*illustrated*). This was a Laforey Class Torpedo Boat Destroyer and was one of the last classes of Destroyers completed before the outbreak of the 1st World War. The ship was one of the first of the class to be given double torpedo tubes and geared turbines. HMS "Laforey" served with the 3rd Destroyer Flotilla after completion in 1913. The ship was on convoy duty escorting several freighters to France but struck a mine off the coast of France and sunk on 25 March 1917. Henry lost his life on that day, aged 23 years.

Having been brought up and educated in Hailsham, the name and rank of "*Seaman H.W. Hollibone*" appears on the Hailsham Boys School Memorial board. His name is also shown on the 'Roll of Honour' printed in the parish magazine and on the Memorial board in St Mary's Church. His name is also on the Chatham Naval Memorial. As apparently being a member of the Weslyan congregation, known to them as Walter, his name is commemorated on the Memorial tablet in Hailsham Methodist Church,

Part Two – The Great War: 1914-18

Jackson, Robert H.

Rank	Regiment	Age at Death
Lance Corporal	Royal Sussex	18yrs

Robert Harold Jackson was born in Hailsham in 1899, the son of Robert and Elizabeth Jackson (*nee Shearman*). In 1911, Robert, then shown as aged 12 years old, was still at Hailsham Council School and living with his parents, at 'Clydesdale', London Road, Hailsham together with one brother and two sisters. His parents later moved to 'Avondale', Union (now Hawks) Road, Hailsham.

In September 1914, Robert enlisted at Hailsham Recruiting Office into the Cyclist Battalion, 2/6th (Territorial) Royal Sussex Regiment (*Service No: TF/265312*) where he later rose to become a Lance Corporal. He served with the Indian Expeditionary Force at Bangalore from August 1915. He saw fighting on the North-West Frontier and also on the Afghan Frontier. He died on 9th October 1917 in hospital in Lahore from pericarditis, contracted whilst on active service. He is buried at Lahore and is commemorated on the Karachi War Memorial in Pakistan.

In December 1917, In Rev F. Clyde Harvey reported in his 'Parish Newsletter': -

"*Robert Harold Jackson, Lance Corporal, was well known in our Church. He was confirmed here. He joined the Cyclist Corps at Brighton in 1914. Nothing would keep him away. He contracted serious illness in two campaigns on the Indian Frontier and died in Hospital at Lahore and was buried there, all the battalion attending.*"

Having been brought up and educated at Hailsham, the name and rank of "*Lance Corporal R.H. Jackson*" appears on the Hailsham Boys School Memorial board. His name also appears in the 'Roll of Honour' printed in the parish magazine as well as the Memorial board in St Mary's Church, Hailsham.

בּ בּ בּ בּ בּ בּ בּ בּ בּ בּ

Jones, William J.

Rank	Regiment	Age at Death
Private	Royal Sussex	22yrs

William James Jones was born in Hailsham in 1894, the son of William Jones. In 1901, William then aged 7 years, was a schoolboy living with his widowed father William Jones, at 'Laurel Cottage' Hailsham. Ten years later, he was still at "Laurel Cottage" with his widowed father and was employed as a nurseryman gardener.

William was in the Territorials at the start of the war and enlisted at the Herstmonceux Recruiting Office into the Royal Sussex Regiment where he served as a Private in the 11th Battalion (*Service No: SD/607*). He was killed in action fighting on the Ancre (Hamel), in one of the battles on the Somme, on 3rd September 1916, aged 22 years. On the same day, his Hailsham comrade, Ernest Atkins, also lost his life. William is buried in Ancre British Cemetery, which contains the graves of 2,540 British soldiers, 1335 of whom are unknown. (*Grave Ref: III. D. 37*)

This action on the Somme was the second of the three great attempts to wrest the town of Beaucourt from the Germans. At the time of his death, his father had remarried and moved to Gordon Place, Hailsham.

Having been brought up and educated in Hailsham, the name and rank of "*Private W.J. Jones*" appears on the Hailsham Boys School Memorial Board. His name also appears in the 'Roll of Honour' printed in the parish magazine as well as on the Memorial board in St Mary's Church.

His death is also commemorated on his father's grave in Hailsham Cemetery (*Grave space D176*)

ꙅꙅꙅꙅꙅꙅꙅꙅꙅꙅ

Kerridge, Charles D.

Rank	Regiment	Age at Death
Private	London (Artists Rifles)	30yrs

Charles Duncan Kerridge was born in Hailsham in September 1887, the son of William and Annie Kerridge. In 1891, Charles was living in Market Square, Hailsham, aged 3 years old along with three brothers and two sisters. His father was shown as an upholsterer. By 1911, the family had moved and Charles, then aged 23 years was still living with his parents, two brothers and three sisters in 7/9/11 High Street, Hailsham. He is shown as being employed as a shop assistant in the furniture trade probably at his father's furniture shop at this address.

Charles enlisted in December 1916 at the age of 29 years and 3 months at Eastbourne Recruiting Office into the London Regiment and gave his address as 7 High Street, Hailsham. He was 5ft 9¾ ins high with no distinguishing marks and classified as 'A' fit. He served as a Private (*Service No: 763932*) in the 28th (County of London) Battalion (Artists Rifles). This Regiment was originally raised in 1859 from a group of painters, sculptors, musicians, etc, as part of the great Volunteer Corps movement that grew rapidly in that year in response to a threat of invasion by Napoleon III. Having completed his basic training, Charles was posted as part of the British Expeditionary Force to France on 20th March 1917.

On 30th October 1917, only seven months after he had been posted, Charles Kerridge was killed in action as part of the ongoing offensive near Ypres, known as Passchendaele. He was aged 30 years. Initially he was officially reported as 'missing' but his death was later confirmed. His personal effects consisting of just his pipe and his pocket book were returned to his father in January 1918. His name is commemorated on The Tyne Cot Memorial, Belgium, which records the names of 8,365 unidentified soldiers (*Memorial Ref: Panel 153*).

His death is also commemorated by an inscription on his parent's grave in Hailsham Cemetery (*Grave space B188*). Having been brought up and educated at Hailsham, the name and rank of *"Rifleman C.D. Kerridge"* appears on the Hailsham Boys School Memorial board. His name also appears on the Memorial board in St Mary's Church, Hailsham as well as in the 'Roll of Honour' printed earlier in the parish magazine.

囚囚囚囚囚囚囚囚囚囚

Kibblewhite, Arthur W.

Rank	Regiment	Age at Death
Private Private	(1) Royal Sussex (2) Royal Fusiliers	24yrs

Arthur William Kibblewhite was born in Hailsham in 1894, the son of Arthur and Flora Kibblewhite. In 1901, the family were living at 15 North Street, Hailsham and he was shown as being William. In 1911, Arthur then aged 17 years was still at home with his parents, Arthur and Flora at 17 North Street, Hailsham together with his one sister. He was then employed as a milk boy. Subsequently he worked as a blacksmith for Messrs T. Rich and Sons, builder and contractor of South Road and High Street, Hailsham. He was a member of the Hailsham Brotherhood.

Arthur was living in Hailsham at the start of the war but it was at the Hastings Recruiting Office in January 1915 that he initially enlisted into the Royal Sussex Regiment (*Service No: G/6374*). He subsequently transferred to the Royal Fusiliers (City of London Regiment) where he served as a Private (*Service No: 60651*) with the 7th Battalion, 63rd Royal Naval Division. He went to the Front in France in 1916 and was wounded once and gassed once. He was initially posted as missing on 21 August 1918 but two months later it was officially confirmed that he had been killed in action on that date. He was aged 24 years. He is buried at Achiet Le Grand Communal Cemetery Extension, Pas de Calais, in France (*Grave Ref: Sp. Mem.5*). This cemetery is south of Arras and contains over 1,400 commemorations.

Having been brought up and educated in Hailsham, the name and rank of "*Private A.W. Kibblewhite*" appears on the Hailsham Boys School Memorial board. His name also appears on the Memorial board in St Mary's Church, Hailsham as well as in the 'Roll of Honour' printed in the parish magazine. Being, apparently, a member of the Weslyan congregation, he is also commemorated on the Memorial tablet in Hailsham Methodist Church.

His war service earned him both the British and Victory Medals.

Part Two – The Great War: 1914-18

Knight, Alfred F.

Rank	Regiment	Age at Death
Rifleman	London	31yrs

Alfred Freeman Knight was born at Hailsham in 1887, the youngest son of Ambrose and Mary Anne Knight. In 1891, the family were living at 2 Albert Place, Hailsham and his father was shown as a butcher. One of his brothers was Charles Henry Knight who was to be killed in the war twelve months before him. Unlike Charles, Alfred continued to live in Hailsham until he joined up. In 1901, the family had moved to 5 Elmsdown Place, Hailsham and Alfred aged 14 years had a job as a telegraph messenger. In 1911, Alfred Knight, then aged 24 years, was boarding with Henry and Esther Whatman at 18 Bellbanks Road, Hailsham and was employed as a postman at the Post Office.

Alfred enlisted in London into the London Regiment. He served as a Rifleman (*Service No: 371255*) in the 8th Battalion, Post Office Rifles, which was attached to the 17th Battalion. He was wounded whilst serving in France & Flanders and subsequently died of his wounds on 31 January 1918. He was buried at Bur Rocquiney Equancourt Road British Cemetery, Manancourt (*Grave Ref: IX.E.24*).

Rocquigny and Equancourt are two villages in the Somme Department of France near to Etricourt. This village was occupied by Commonwealth troops at the beginning of April 1917 during the German withdrawal to the Hindenburg Line. It was lost on the 23 March 1918 when the Germans advanced, but regained at the beginning of September. It is probably during this last action that Alfred Knight sustained the wounds that lead to his death.

Having been brought up and educated in Hailsham, the name and rank of "*Rifleman A.F. Knight*" appears on the Hailsham Boys School Memorial board. His name also appears on the Memorial board in St Mary's Church, Hailsham as well as in the 'Roll of Honour' printed earlier in the parish magazine. Being, apparently, a member of the Weslyan congregation, he is also commemorated on the Memorial tablet in Hailsham Methodist Church.

ᘇ ᘇ ᘇ ᘇ ᘇ ᘇ ᘇ ᘇ ᘇ ᘇ

Part Two – The Great War: 1914-18

Knight, Charles H.

Rank	Regiment	Age at Death
Corporal	Australian Infantry	34yrs

Charles Henry Knight was born in Hailsham in 1883, the second son of Ambrose and Mary Anne Knight of Hailsham. In 1891, the family were living at 2 Albert Place, Hailsham and his father was shown as a butcher. One of his brothers was Alfred Knight who was to be killed in the war twelve months later than him. In 1901, the family had moved to 5 Elmsdown Place, Hailsham and Charles, aged 17 years was shown as a grocer's assistant. By 1911, Charles had left home and was a boarder at Lyminge, near Folkestone and described as a self-employed grocer. He subsequently married and emigrated to Australia where Service records show him as the husband of Dorothy Knight of Subiaco, Western Australia.

He enlisted into the Australian Infantry (*Service No: 7259*) in the 11th Battalion, 1st Australian Division and rose to become a Corporal. He was killed in action on 27th September 1917, aged 34 years. His death is commemorated on The Menin Gate Memorial, Ypres in Belgium (*Memorial Ref: Panel 7; 17 to 29*).

Having been educated at Hailsham, the name and rank of *"Corporal C.H. Knight"* appears on the Hailsham Boys School Memorial board. His name also appears on the Memorial board in St Mary's Church, Hailsham as well as in the 'Roll of Honour' printed earlier in the parish magazine. Being, apparently, a member of the Weslyan congregation, he is also commemorated on the Memorial tablet in Hailsham Methodist Church.

Part Two – The Great War: 1914-18

Larkin, William J.

Rank	Regiment	Age at Death
Private	Royal Sussex	26yrs

William John Larkin was born in Shoreham in 1890, the son of William and Agnes Larkin. In 1911, William, aged 11 years was living with his parents near Malling in Kent and his father was employed as a coachman.

William enlisted at the Brighton Recruiting Office into the Royal Sussex Regiment. He served as a Private (*Service No: G/16237*) in the 12th Battalion, 29th Division. He was killed in action on 10th October 1916, aged 26 years, in action described as being part of the Battles of the Somme: Fighting on the Ancre (Hamel). He is buried in Euston Road Cemetery, Colincamps in the Somme Department of France (*Grave Ref: IV.M.7*). His death is also commemorated on the Rottingdean War Memorial in Sussex.

There is no 'obvious' sign of either him or his parents being in Hailsham at the time of the 1911 census. However, Thomas and Richard Larkin had a saddler's business in Hailsham High Street, which ran up until 1956 and it is more than possible that William was related to this family and might even have been working there or at least working in the town.

His name appears in the 'Roll of Honour' in the parish magazine as well as being shown on the Memorial board in St Mary's Church. In addition, being, apparently, a member of the Weslyan congregation, he is also commemorated on the Memorial tablet in Hailsham Methodist Church. This provides further evidence that he was either working or living in Hailsham before he joined up.

฿฿฿฿฿฿฿฿฿฿฿

Part Two – The Great War: 1914-18

Leeson, Albert E.

Rank	Regiment	Age at Death
Private	London	19yrs

Albert Edward Leeson was born in Stepney, London in 1899, the youngest son of Benjamin, a police constable in the Metropolitan police, and Elizabeth Leeson. In 1911, Albert, then aged 12 years, was living with his mother and siblings in Stepney, London and going to school in Stepney. There is a slight 'mystery' about Albert's father as he was not shown on either the 1901 or 1911 census returns. It is probable that he had died as, in 1901, Albert's mother, Elizabeth, is shown as a widow. However in 1911 she states that she is married and has been so for 19 years.

Albert enlisted at the Stepney Recruiting Office into the 6th London Regiment (*Service No: 323425*) and served as a Private. He subsequently transferred into the 22nd Battalion (City of London) the Queen's, (*Service No: 698105*). He served in France and Flanders.

Operation 'Michael' was a German offensive between 21 March and 3 April 1915 under General Ludendorff. Three German armies were deployed against the British Third and Fifth armies on the former Somme battlefield between Arras and La Fere. After initial gains, the German assault eventually lost momentum. When it was halted, the British had sustained some 163,000 casualties and the French 77,000. Albert was killed during the very early days of Operation 'Michael', when the fighting was at its height, on 23rd March 1918. His death is commemorated on the Arras Memorial, as he has no known grave (*Memorial Ref: Bay 9 or 10*).

There is only one sign of Albert either living, working or having a direct connection with Hailsham and that is through his brother, Benjamin. Ben, as he preferred to be called, was landlord of the Crown Hotel in the High Street, Hailsham sometime during the years 1919 to 1921 (*See advertisement that only appeared in the 1920-21 street directory*).

Albert's name appears in the 'Roll of Honour' printed in the parish magazine as well as on the Memorial board in St Mary's Church.

Part Two – The Great War: 1914-18

Levett, Joseph R.

Rank	Regiment	Age at Death
Corporal	Royal Sussex	26yrs

Joseph Richard Levett, usually known as 'Joe', was born at Hailsham in 1894, the fourth son of Benjamin and Rebecca Levett. In 1901, the family were living at Foxhall, Hailsham. His father was an estate woodsman and Joseph had four elder brothers and a sister. In 1911, Joseph then aged 17 years, was living in the family home at 86 South Road, Hailsham and he now had five brothers. He was employed as a twine spinner at Burfield's Rope and Twine factory in South Road, Hailsham.

Joseph was still working in the twine department of Burfield's when, on 15 October 1912 aged 19 years and 3 months, he joined the Territorial army for a four-year term. When the war started, he enlisted at Hailsham into the 5th Battalion Cinque Ports Royal Sussex Regiment where he served as a Private (*Service No: TF/202042*). Whilst serving in the forces, he played football for the Battalion team. In February 1915 he was posted to France and served as part of the Expeditionary Force. He was promoted to Lance Corporal on 1 September 1916 and to Corporal on 19 February 1918. He was wounded several times in action, once at Abeluq in 1916. He also saw service on the Italian Front. He continued to serve until 3 March 1919 when he returned to England and was demobbed on 3 April 1919. He returned to his home in Hailsham and was awarded the 1914 Star and the British War and Victory Medals.

He took up his former trade as twine spinner but this time with Green Brothers. He was a keen member of the Hailsham Cricket Club and a prominent and useful member of the Hailsham football Club. Tragically, he died as a result of the war wounds he had sustained, at his home, 86 South Road, Hailsham on 8 July 1920, aged 26 years. He is buried in Hailsham Cemetery in one of the ten WWI graves maintained by the Commonwealth War Graves Commission (*Grave space 1806*).

His name appears on the Memorial board in St Mary's Church, Hailsham as well as being in the 'Roll of Honour' printed earlier in the parish magazine. Being a former employee of Burfield's Rope and Twine factory, his name also appears in their 'Roll of Honour' written in Burfield's Factory Record and Visitors book, under the heading "*The Factory Recorder*".

ﭏﭏﭏﭏﭏﭏﭏﭏﭏﭏ

Part Two – The Great War: 1914-18

Limon, Henry

Rank	Regiment	Age at Death
Private	Honourable Artillery Co	25yrs

Henry Limon was born at Burgh in Lincolnshire in 1892, the only son of Henry and Fanny Limon. The family moved to Hailsham in about 1894 when Henry was two years old. He was educated at the Eastbourne Municipal School and then the Westminster School of Pharmacy. In 1911, Henry, then aged 19 years, was living with his parents and the family had moved to 25 High Street, Hailsham. His father was described as a pharmacist's manager working at a pharmacy whilst Henry was a pharmacist's assistant, the same profession as his father. He was apprenticed to Mr Arthur Mills, chemist, of Eastbourne. He gained his certificate of membership of the Pharmaceutical Society of Great Britain after joining up. At one time, he was a racing member of the 'famous' North Road Cycling Club and, in 1914, secured the trophy for riding 192½ miles in the 12 hours road handicap.

In December 1915, Henry enlisted at the Armoury House in London into the Honourable Artillery Company where he served as a Private (*Service No: 6511*) in the 2nd Battalion, 7th Division. He went to the Front in October 1915 and served in France and Flanders. He remained fighting on the Western Front on the Somme.

The village of Beauport-Hamel on the Somme was first attacked on 1 July 1916 by the 29th Division but without success. A further attack took place on 3 September 1916 but it was not until the middle of November 1916 that the village was finally captured. The Germans finally withdrew to the Hindenburg Line in the spring of 1917. Henry Limon was killed during this action on 12 January 1917 aged 25 years. He is buried in Ancre British Cemetery, Beaumont Hamel, in the Somme Department of France (*Grave Ref: VII.C.39*).

St Mary's parish magazine reported: - "*Private H. Limon who used to attend our Church and was confirmed here and was a Communicant, died bravely for his country and his fellow men at Beaumont Hamel. He did his best; he gave his life.*"

His name appears in the 'Roll of Honour' printed in the parish magazine as well as on the Memorial board in St Mary's Church, Hailsham. According to the Sussex Express, in his later years, he was better known in Eastbourne, rather than Hailsham.

בּ בּ בּ בּ בּ בּ בּ בּ בּ בּ

Lusted, Alfred T. (DCM)

Rank	Regiment	Age at Death
Sergeant	Royal Sussex	27yrs

Alfred Thomas Lusted was born at Hailsham in 1895, the son of Alfred and Sarah Lusted. In 1911, Alfred then aged 16 years was living with his parents at 30 Bell Banks Road, Hailsham along with one brother. He was employed as a mat maker at Burfields Rope & Twine factory.

It is not known when or where he enlisted but he joined the Royal Sussex Regiment (*Service No: 320496*) where he served as a Private in the 16th Battalion. He rose to the rank of Sergeant and was later awarded the Distinguished Conduct Medal. His Citation in the London Gazette dated 11 March 1920 reads as follows:

> *"For gallantry and devotion to duty, both in the outpost line at Sinjil, Palestine and in France. Especially so in front of Merville in July 1918; he by his daring leadership brought excellent results, including valuable information most helpful to the advance of the battalion."*

The Factory Record and Visitors Book for Burfield & Son, 1909 to 1926, records the names and details of their employees who served their King and Country in the Great War. Written in pencil, almost as an afterthought, at the bottom of the first page is the name of *"Lusted, Alf"*. The column for the name of the regiment shows *"Sx, yes"* (*sic*), which indicated that he was in the Sussex Regiment. The remarks column shows *"Died 1921"*, but this turned out to be one year adrift. As well as his DCM, his war service earned him the Victory Medal and the British Medal.

Alfred, described as a labourer, died at his home, 75a South Road, Hailsham on 26 March 1922, nearly four years after the end of the war. He was buried in Hailsham cemetery (*Grave No: 1880*).

The late date of his death explains why his name does not appear either in the 'Roll of Honour' printed in the parish magazine, or the Memorial board in St Mary's Church, Hailsham, or on the Boys School Memorial board where he was probably educated. The award of his DCM was announced in March 1920 but is not shown on the war Memorial in the High Streetl in Hailsham, unlike that for Frederick Marrillier. The most probable reason for this is that the name of Alfred T. Lusted was one of the eleven names added to the Memorial later on (*see page 10*), and that there was physically no room to include mention of his Decoration.

(*see page 10*)

ꙥ ꙥ ꙥ ꙥ ꙥ ꙥ ꙥ ꙥ ꙥ ꙥ

Part Two – The Great War: 1914-18

Marillier, F.C.J., DCM

Rank	Regiment	Age at Death
Second Lieutenant	Royal Sussex	27yrs

Frederick Charles Jennens Marillier was born at Hastings, about 1888, the son of Ernest and Alice Marillier. In 1901, Frederick, his parents and younger sister were living at Jubilee House, Magham Down. Frederick's father was an accomplished artist/life insurance agent whilst his mother was a music teacher. Frederick grew up in Hailsham, living with his parents in North Street, trained as a teacher and became very popular later as an assistant master at the Hailsham Boys School. He interested himself in the Boy Scout movement, and was a Sergeant in the Territorials (5th Cinque Ports Battalion, Royal Sussex Regiment). He also played football for Hailsham Second XI. He eventually decided on a military career. In 1910 at Chichester, he joined the Royal Sussex Regiment, 2nd Battalion as a Private but with the determination (as he told Mr Towler, the former headmaster of his school) to rise to the rank of Captain. He did gain rapid promotion and eventually rose to the rank of Second Lieutenant with the 2nd Battalion.

In mid 1914, St Mary's parish magazine reported that a Mr Mills had received the following letter from Mr Marillier:- *"I have gone through the whole campaign from Mons onward, without mishap, except slight shrapnel bits. I have received my Commission and look forward to seeing Hailsham again. Please remember me to my old friends."*

Frederick was tragically killed in "fierce action", a few months after above the letter was written, at Bodmin Copse, near Ypres in Belgium on 30th October 1914 aged 27 years. His death is commemorated on the Menin Gate Memorial at Ypres. The Eastbourne Gazette made the following report in their issue of 11th November 1914.

"The late Lieutenant Marillier, of the Royal Sussex Regiment, was one of the two Royal Sussex non-commissioned officers out of the twenty-three of the British Expeditionary Force to whom the King approved the grant of the medal for Distinguished Service in the field and for acts of gallantry and devotion to duty. The "London Gazette" of Friday last contained the following announcement: -"Sergeant (now Second-Lieutenant F.C.J. Marillier, 2nd Battalion Royal Sussex Regiment) led a party on the night of 1st October and successfully filled one of the enemy's trenches".

Having been a teacher at Hailsham, the name of "*Lieutenant F.C.J. Marillier, DCM*" appears on the School Memorial board. His name also appears in the 'Roll of Honour' printed in the parish magazine as well as on the Memorial board in St Mary's Church.

ഇഇഇഇഇഇഇഇഇഇ

Part Two – The Great War: 1914-18

Maryan, Ernest

Rank	Regiment	Age at Death
Private	Royal Sussex	31yrs

Ernest Maryan was born at Hailsham around 1883, the son of Thomas Maryan, a twine maker, and his wife, Ellen. In 1891, Ernest, then aged 8 years, was living near Stoney Lane in Hailsham with his parents, one elder brother and three sisters. In 1911, Ernest is shown as single and still living with his parents, this time at 23 Garfield Road, Hailsham. His occupation is given as being a soldier.

He enlisted at Eastbourne as a Regular Soldier into the Royal Sussex Regiment and served as a Private (*Service No: L/7419*) with the 2nd Battalion, 1st Division. He served in the Western European theatre of the war as part of the British Expeditionary Force that took part in the first battle of Ypres. In this battle, from 24 October 1914 onward, fighting was continuous, both day and night, along the Ypres salient in conditions dominated by mud and winter cold. Six additional German armies moved into a gap between the fourth and sixth Allied armies, supported by a very heavy concentration of artillery. The Germans outnumbered the Allied troops by two to one. In the heaviest period of fighting to date, between 30 October and 4 November 1914, the Allied troops were driven back. Ernest was killed during this action in the First Battle of Ypres on 1 November 1914. His death is commemorated on the Menin Gate Memorial at Ypres, Belgium (*Memorial Ref: Panel 20*).

Having been educated in Hailsham, the name and rank of "*Private E. Maryan*" appears on the Hailsham Boys School Memorial board. His name also appears on the Memorial board in St Mary's Church, Hailsham as well as in the 'Roll of Honour' printed earlier in the parish magazine.

ᘛᘛᘛᘛᘛᘛᘛᘛᘛᘛ

Maryan, Wilfred J.

Rank	Regiment	Age at Death
Gunner	Royal Field Artillery	31yrs

Wilfred James Maryan was born at Hailsham in 1891, the elder son of James H. Maryan, described as a 'commercial traveller', and Mary his wife. The family were then living at 6 Wellington Villa, Hailsham. Wilfred was educated at Southdown College in Eastbourne. In 1907, he joined Burfields, rope and twine factory as a clerk. In 1911, Wilfred, now aged 20 years, was living at his parent's home at 11 London Road, Hailsham along with his brother and sister. His father, James, is now shown as a traveller and joint managing director of a manufacturing firm and this, of course, is the well-known firm of Burfields, rope and twine manufacturer. On the census, Wilfred is shown as manufacturing clerk in his father's business but he later became a commercial traveller for the firm covering the Kent, Hampshire and Surrey areas.

Wilfred subsequently married Mercy Catt and they lived at "Ambleside", Summerheath Road, Hailsham and had two children, a son and a daughter. Wilfred described himself as being a commercial traveller and was working at Burfields in 1917 when he enlisted.

He joined the Signal Section of the Royal Field Artillery and served as a Gunner (*Service No: 226263*). He served in the trenches mainly in France and Belgium and was in France when the Armstice was signed. Whilst there, he contracted septic poisoning and he never really recovered from the effects of this. On demobilisation, he returned to Burfields but still continued to suffer from the poisoning. He was described as being very popular with the other employees in the Factory. He eventually died of his illness at his home "Ambleside" in Hailsham on 17 May 1922 leaving a widow and two young children, a boy and a girl. He was buried in Hailsham Cemetery (*Grave space 493*).

Having died in 1922, several years after the war officially ended, his name does not appear either in the 'Roll of Honour' printed in the parish magazine, nor on the Memorial board in St Mary's Church, Hailsham which was unveiled in 1919. His name is shown on the 'Roll of Honour' written in Burfield's day book under the heading "*The Factory Recorder*" with the comment '*Died 17/5/1922*'.

ꛯꛯꛯꛯꛯꛯꛯꛯꛯ

Part Two – The Great War: 1914-18

Matthews, David H.

Rank	Regiment	Age at Death
Private	Royal Sussex	24yrs

David H. Matthews was born at Hailsham around 1893, the seventh son of George and Mary Matthews who finished up with having a family of twelve, ten sons and two daughters living out of fifteen. In 1911, David, then aged 18 years, is still at home with his parents, four brothers and one sister, living at 'The Pines', South Road, Hailsham. David's occupation is shown as being a matting weaver, employed at the Rope Works. By October 1914, the family had moved to 8 Windsor Road, Hailsham and David was working at Messrs Scotts' Nurseries at Eastbourne. He is described as being a keen sportsman and played both cricket and football for the Hailsham teams. Latterly, owing to an injury to a knee, he was unable to play football in the field but kept goal instead.

David enlisted at the Herstmonceux Recruiting Office on 11th October 1914 into the Royal Sussex Regiment and served as a Private (*Service No: SD/616*) in the 11th Battalion, 39th Division. He went to the Front in March 1915. He was killed in action on 21 October 1916 but it was many anxious months of waiting after his parents were informed that he was 'missing' before they received an official notification of his death. He is buried in Grandcourt Road Cemetery in the Somme Department of France (*Grave Ref: Row B. Grave 46*).

The village of Grandcourt was reached by the 36th (Ulster) Division on the 1st July 1916 but was not taken until 7th February 1917 when patrols of the 63rd (Royal Naval) Division found it deserted. Grandcourt Road Cemetery was made in the spring of 1917 when the Ancre battlefield was cleared. Over 250, WWI casualties are commemorated in this site and, of these, over one-fifth are unidentified. All fell in the period July 1916, to February 1917.

Having been brought up and educated at Hailsham, the name and rank of "*Private D. Matthews*" appears on the Hailsham Boys School Memorial board. His name also appears on the Memorial board in St Mary's Church, Hailsham as well as in the 'Roll of Honour' printed in the parish magazine in 1918.

ɷɷɷɷɷɷɷɷɷɷ

Matthews, Frederick K.

Rank	Regiment	Age at Death
Sergeant	Royal Engineers	36yrs

Frederick Matthews was born at Hailsham in January 1883, the son of Henry and Caroline Matthews. In 1891, Frederick aged 7 years was living with his parents and his two brothers in the Barrack Ground in Hailsham. In 1901, Frederick aged 17 years was employed as a labourer on the Railway and was living with his parents and now three brothers at 73 South Road, Hailsham. In December 1904, Frederick married Lillian Sargent who came from Ninfield and their family subsequently consisted of three boys and one girl. In 1911, he and his family were living at 71 South Road, Hailsham, (next door to his parents) and Frederick was working as a 'navvy' for the Railway Company.

In October 1914, aged 30 years, being then employed as a gas fitter for the Eastbourne Gas Company, he enlisted at Eastbourne for a period of one year into the Territorials (*Service No 993*) as part of Home Defence. Unfortunately, despite initially being declared fit, he was discharged 24 days later as being medically unfit.

In December 1915, he enlisted at Eastbourne into the Royal Engineers. He served as a sapper (*Service No 180928*) and was posted to the Railway Troops Depot as part of the M.E.F. (Mediterranean Expeditionary Force). He later transferred to the E.E.F. (Egyptian Expeditionary Force) as part of the Railway Operating Division (*Service No WR/287428*) and served in Egypt as a platelayer. His service continued after the war had ended and in October 1919, he was promoted to the rank of Sergeant. He died in Alexandria on 28 December 1919 whilst trying to keep warm on a cold desert night.

The official report states: *"he was found in the Station building at Tilul. The room had been made practically airtight by the shutting of both windows and the closing (by locking) of the door. Within four feet of the body, a burnt out open coke brazier was found. ..... Death had been caused by Carbon Monoxide Poisoning, the gas being generated by the coke brazier. Owing to the closing of the windows and door, the gas had reached sufficient concentration to cause death. The death was, in my opinion, accidental."* He was buried in Kantara War Memorial cemetery in Egypt (*Grave Ref: B.104*).

Because of the late date of his death, his name does not appear on the Hailsham Boys School Memorial board. For the same reason, it does not appear either in the 'Roll of Honour' printed in the parish magazine or on the Memorial board in St Mary's Church, Hailsham.

স্থ স্থ স্থ স্থ স্থ স্থ স্থ স্থ স্থ স্থ

Part Two – The Great War: 1914-18

Milward, Frank

Rank	Regiment	Age at Death
Private	Essex	29yrs

Frank Milward was born at Hailsham around 1887, the son of Thomas Milward, a bricklayer, and his wife, Harriett. In 1891, Frank was aged 4 years old and at home in South Road, Hailsham with his parents, his two brothers and two sisters. In 1901, he was still living in the family home at 44 South Road, Hailsham but this time the records show that his father had died and there were three other brothers and one sister still at home with their widowed mother. At age 14 years, Frank was employed as a rope spinner. For whatever reason, Frank does not appear on the 1911 census. The rest of his family have been split up with two brothers being adopted and living in Hailsham, one living and working in Eastbourne and his one sister living and working in Hailsham.

Frank was still living in Hailsham when he enlisted at the Hastings Recruiting Office into the Essex Regiment. He served as a Private (*Service No: 17095*) in the 11th Battalion, 6th Division in France and Flanders, the Western European theatre of war. He was killed in action during the long drawn out War of Attrition on the Somme. He died on 27 September 1916, aged 29 years.

His death is commemorated on The Thiepval Memorial, which is the Memorial to the Missing of the Somme (*Memorial Ref: Pier & Face 10D*). It bears the names of more than 72,000 officers and  men of the United Kingdom and South African forces who died in the Somme sector before 20 March 1918 and have no known grave. Over 90% of those commemorated died between July and November 1916.

Having been brought up and educated in Hailsham, the name and rank of "*Private F. Milward*" appears on the Hailsham Boys School Memorial board. Whilst his name does not appear in the 'Roll of Honour' printed in the parish magazine in 1918, it does appear on the Memorial board in St Mary's Church, Hailsham.

୪୪୪୪୪୪୪୪୪୪୪

Part Two – The Great War: 1914-18

Morse, Corrie

Rank	Regiment	Age at Death
Private	Royal Fusiliers	19yrs

Corrie Morse was born in Hailsham in 1898, the son of Sidney and Alice Morse. In 1901, Corrie, aged 3 years was living with his parents and three siblings in Eastwell Place, Hailsham. Ten years later, Corrie then aged 13 years, is at school, living with his parents, Sidney, a watchmaker's assistant and Alice his wife, plus his brother and two sisters at Bridge House, Hailsham. His father was probably working in the family watchmaker business of J. Morse, situated at 55 High Street, Hailsham. As a young man, Corrie was described as being well known in Hailsham and particularly in Hampden Park where he was managing the Hampden Park Branch of the London, City and Midland Bank. He was a member of the Hailsham Congregational Church.

He was still living at Bridge House, Hailsham when he enlisted in April 1916 at the Eastbourne Recruiting Office. He joined the Royal Fusiliers (City of London) Regiment where he served as a Private (*Service No: 23694*) with the 26th Battalion. He subsequently transferred to the 11th Battalion of the same Regiment, still as a Private (*Service No: 50375*) and served in the Western European theatre of war. He was killed in action, whilst serving in France & Flanders on 17th February 1917, aged 19 years. He is buried in Regina Trench Cemetery, Grandcourt, France. (*Grave Ref: VII.E.5*)

On 1 July 1916, the first day of the Battle of the Somme, Grandcourt village was reached by the 36th (Ulster) Division, but it was not until the German withdrawal to the Hindenburg Line, early in February 1917, that it was occupied by patrols of the Howe Battalion, Royal Naval Division. Regina Trench was a German earthwork, captured for a time by the 5th Canadian Brigade on 1 October 1916, attacked again by the 1st and 3rd Canadian Divisions on 8 October, taken in part by the 18th and 4th Canadian Divisions on 21 October, and finally cleared by the 4th Canadian Division on 11 November 1916. It was probably during the action that led to the German withdrawal that Corrie Morse lost his life.

Having been brought up and educated in Hailsham, the name and rank of "*Private C. Morse*" appears on the Hailsham Boys School Memorial board. His name also appears in the 'Roll of Honour' printed in the parish magazine in 1918 as well as on the Memorial board in St Mary's Church, Hailsham.

෴෴෴෴෴෴෴෴෴෴

Part Two – The Great War: 1914-18

Murrell, George

Rank	Regiment	Age at Death
Sergeant	Royal Field Artillery	21yrs

George Murrell was born at Iden in Kent about September 1896, the son of William and Catherine Murrell. By 1901, George was aged 5 years, the family had moved to Hailsham and were living at Harebeating Farm. His father William was employed as a bricklayer. In the 1911 census, George, is shown as being aged 15 years, employed as a milk carrier and was living with his parents and one brother in Hempstead Lane, Hailsham. He subsequently worked for Mr W.H. Lawrence, a grocer in Hailsham. He was a Corporal in the Hailsham Territorials when war broke out. He was also a member of the Hailsham Brotherhood and, as a boy, attended the Weslyan Sunday Schools.

George enlisted at Eastbourne into the Sussex Battery, 8th Home Counties Brigade, Royal Field Artillery in November 1911 for a four year period. He stated that he was 17 years and 2 months old but he had actually inflated his age by 2 years which was never found out. When he enlisted, he was living at Thatched Cottage, Hempstead Lane, Hailsham. He described himself as a dairyman working for Mr A. More and was recorded as being 5ft 2½ ins tall. He signed on as a driver (*Service No: 215*), trained at Lark Hill and was promoted acting Corporal in January 1913. At the end of October 1914, he was posted to India. He was promoted to substantive Bombardier and then to Acting Sergeant in March 1916. He reported sick at Rawalpindi hospital, in India in April 1916 and was admitted to hospital where he was diagnosed with tuberculosis. In August 1916, he was sent back to England on the hospital ship, "*Delta*". He was eventually discharged with a 'very good' character reference under Para. 392 (xvi) Kings Regulations on 23 November 1916 from the Royal Hospital in Chelsea and awarded a pension of 20 shillings per week as a single man. He gave his trade as being a grocer's assistant and that he intended to live in Hailsham where his mother then lived at 13 South Road. At his medical review in Eastbourne the following March, it was stated that he had not worked since his discharge and had not been able to return to his former employer. George died in Hailsham on 11 October 1917, aged 21 years and was buried in Hailsham Cemetery (*Grave space: 461 – No headstone*).

George was educated locally and the name and rank of "*Sergeant G. Murrell*" appears on the Hailsham Boys School Memorial board. George is also shown on the Memorial board in the Methodist Church, Hailsham, which gives his Regiment as being the Royal Field Artillery. The 'Roll of Honour' printed in St Mary's parish magazine shows him as a Sergeant in the R.F.A. and his name also appears on the Memorial board in St Mary's Church, Hailsham. Being a member of the Weslyan congregation, George is also commemorated on the Memorial tablet in Hailsham Methodist Church.

ꙥ ꙥ ꙥ ꙥ ꙥ ꙥ ꙥ ꙥ ꙥ ꙥ

Part Two – The Great War: 1914-18

Noakes, Percy J.

Rank	Regiment	Age at Death
Private	Royal Sussex	24yrs

Percy John Noakes was born at Berwick in late 1893, the eldest son of Alfred Noakes, a postman, and his wife, Harriett. In 1901, Percy, aged 7 years was living in the family home at Upper Horsebridge with his two younger brothers. Ten years later, Percy then aged 17 years and single, was employed as a farm labourer. He was living with his parents, together with his two brothers and three sisters at 2 South View, Leap Cross, Hellingly. Some time later, his parents moved to 1 Eastwell Place, Hailsham. Before joining up, he worked for Mr Tom Lade at Town Farm, Hailsham.

Percy enlisted at the Hastings Recruiting Office into the Royal Sussex Regiment. He served as a Private (*Service No: SD/2978*) with the 9th Battalion, 24th Division as part of the British Expeditionary Force in the Western European theatre of war. In November 1916, a news article in the Sussex Express shows that both Percy and his two brothers were 'serving their country'. Percy was described as 'wounded', Albert was a Seaman on "*HMS Implacable*" whilst William was a gunner with the Honourable Artillery Company. Percy had actually been wounded by shrapnel in the nose and throat on 3 September 1916 and was sent to a military hospital at Leicester and in December had ten days hospital leave at home with his parents. He went to the Front again in mid May 1916, about three weeks before his death.

Percy saw action in the Battle of Messines Ridge, a high point which had been held and fortified by the Germans since 1914. A new method of attack was needed and the British resolved to dig deep tunnels under the German lines and place mines underneath them. By June 1917, the tunnels were completed and one million pounds of explosive were placed for simultaneous detonation. Following a 17-day concentrated bombardment, on the morning of 7 June 1917, the mines were detonated. The ground shook and the noise was so violent, that it was heard as far away as south east England. Percy lost his life in the aftermath of this engagement. He was officially confirmed as having been killed in action on 11 June 1917 at Messines, aged 24 years. His death is commemorated on the Menin Gate Memorial at Ypres, Belgium (*Memorial Ref: Panel 20*).

Having been brought up and educated at Hailsham, the name and rank of "*Private P.J. Noakes*" appears on the Hailsham Boys School Memorial board. His name also appears in the 'Roll of Honour' printed in the parish magazine in 1919 as well as on the Memorial board in St Mary's Church, Hailsham.

၌၌၌၌၌၌၌၌၌၌

Parsons, David (1)

Rank	Regiment	Age at Death
Private	Royal Sussex	32yrs

David Parsons (*the first of two with this name*) was born in Hailsham about 1884, the youngest son of Henry and Sophia Parsons. In 1891, David was living at 6 Millwalk Cottages, Mill Road, Hailsham, aged 6 years, and living with his five elder brothers, all shown as the children of Henry Parsons, a twine spinner, and Sophia his wife. In 1901, David is shown as aged 17 years and employed as a bricklayer's labourer. He is still living at the family home at 6 Millwalk Cottages in Mill Road, Hailsham but David's father, Henry, still a twine spinner, is now a widower. David was a sportsman. He played for the Hailsham football team and, later in the half back line for the Heathfield United football club. By 1911, Henry's sons have all left home and he is living on his own, still at the same address. In the meantime, David had got married and moved with his wife to Eastbourne where they lived at 16 Sidley Road. They subsequently had three children.

David enlisted at the Eastbourne Recruiting Office into the Royal Sussex Regiment. He served as a Private (*Service No: SD/1427*) in the 12th Battalion, 39th Division as part of the British Expeditionary Force. On enlistment, he stated that his next of kin was living in Hailsham. He was killed in action on 30th June 1916 in the Battle of Boar's Head at Richebourg on the Rue de Bois, which was the same day and action where Nelson Carter and Claude Toye also lost their lives (*Refer to pages 150 – 152 for further details of this action*). This battle was the diversionary attack when Lowther's Lambs went 'over the top' and which was designed, but disastrously failed, to distract attention from the major offensive on the Somme due to start the following day. David's body was never identified and his death is commemorated on the Loos Memorial (*Memorial Ref: Panel 69 to 73*).

Having been brought up and educated in Hailsham, the name and rank of "*Private D. Parsons*" appears on the Hailsham Boys School 'Roll of Honour'. His name also appears on the Memorial board in St Mary's Church, Hailsham although it is not shown in the earlier 'Roll of Honour' printed in the parish magazine.

෨෨෨෨෨෨෨෨෨෨

Parsons, David (2)

Rank	Regiment	Age at Death
Private	Royal Sussex	25yrs

David Parsons (*the second of two with this name*) was born in Hellingly in 1893, the son of Aaron and Annie Parsons. In 1911, David, aged 18 years, was living with his parents, Aaron, a roadman with the County Council, his wife Annie, and three brothers, a sister and a stepbrother at 68 South Road, Hailsham. One of his younger brothers was George who was later also killed in action, almost a year after David was killed. David initially worked in Mr Stephen Boniface's nurseries at Hailsham but later worked at the Duke's Head Hotel at Addlestone in Surrey.

David was called up on the outbreak of war and enlisted at the Hailsham Recruiting Office with the Royal Sussex Regiment and served as a Private (*Service No: TF/240032*) in the 1/5th Battalion, 48th Division. He went to the Front in February 1915. After one month leave in April 1916 he returned to France. He was mortally wounded in the 3rd Battle of Ypres and died on 12th October 1917, aged 24 years. His Commander wrote that "*he was hit by a shell which fell in our lines and he died almost immediately*". David is buried and commemorated in Solferino Farm Cemetery in Belgium (*Grave Ref: I.B.11*).

This cemetery is located to the north-west of the town of Ypres, in France near a village called Brielen. Solferino Farm was given its name by French troops who held this part of the line early in 1915. The cemetery was begun by Commonwealth forces in October 1917 and was used by the units fighting in this sector until August 1918. His

war service earned him the 1915 Star, the Victory medal and also the British War medal.

Having been brought up and educated at Hailsham, the name and rank of "*Private D. Parsons*" appears on the Hailsham Boys School 'Roll of Honour'. His name also appears in the 'Roll of Honour' printed in the parish magazine in 1918 as well as on the Memorial board in St Mary's Church, Hailsham. An inscription for both David and his brother George appears on their parent's grave in Hailsham Cemetery (*Grave space 2235*).

בּ בּ בּ בּ בּ בּ בּ בּ בּ בּ

Part Two – The Great War: 1914-18

Parsons, George

Rank	Regiment	Age at Death
Private	Royal Marines Light Infantry	21yrs

George Parsons was born at Hellingly in 1898, the son of Aaron, a roadman with East Sussex County Council, and Annie, his wife. By 1901, the family had moved to 68 South Road, Hailsham where George, aged 3 had a stepbrother, two brothers and one sister. In 1911, George, then aged 13 years and still at school, was living with his parents, his three brothers, his sister and a step-brother still at 68 South Road, Hailsham. One of his brothers was David Parsons, who was killed in action almost a year before George himself was also killed. George was employed as a porter at Hailsham Railway Station.

George enlisted into the Royal Marines Light Infantry in 1916 at age 18 years. (*Service No: PO/1938*) He served as a Private with the 2nd Royal Marine Battalion, Royal Navy Division. He was killed in action on 8th October 1918 during the capture from the Germans of the small village of Forenville, some 5 kilometers south east of Cambrai. He was buried at the small Forenville Military Cemetery, Nord, in France, which contains 101 burials from WW1 (*Grave Ref: E.4*).

Having been brought up and educated at Hailsham, the name and rank of *"Private G. Parsons"* appears on the Hailsham Boys School 'Roll of Honour'. His name appears in the 'Roll of Honour' printed in the parish magazine in 1918 where he is shown as a *"Private in the 2nd R.M.L.I."* His name is also shown on the Memorial board in St Mary's Church, Hailsham.

An inscription for both George and his brother David appears on their parent's grave in Hailsham Cemetery (*Grave space 2235*).

൝ ൝ ൝ ൝ ൝ ൝ ൝ ൝ ൝ ൝

Part Two – The Great War: 1914-18

Pelling, Ernest A.

Rank	Regiment	Age at Death
Private	Royal Sussex	33yrs

Ernest Alfred Pelling was born in Hailsham in 1884, the son of Thomas Parsons, a farmer with 21 acres, and his wife, Winifred. Thomas was farming at White Dyke, Hailsham. Tragically Ernest's father, Thomas, died within a few years and by 1891, Ernest, aged 7 years, was living with his widowed mother, Winifred, a needlewoman, two elder brothers and a sister at 7 Gordon Place, Hailsham. By 1901, the family had moved to 9 Gordon Road, Hailsham. Ernest was aged 17 years, employed as a cocoa matting weaver and was living with his widowed mother and an elder brother. In 1911, Ernest, shown as aged 26 years, single, was boarding with Frederick and Rose Flint at 128 Ashford Road, Eastbourne and employed as a house porter.

Sometime in the next few years following 1911, Ernest decided to join the army and enlisted into the Royal Sussex Regiment. He enlisted at Eastbourne and served as a Private (*Service No: L/7327*) with the 2nd Battalion as part of the British Expeditionary Force (B.E.F.) His Battalion took part in the First battle of the Aisne in 1914.

The German armies were in retreat following the battle of the Marne and turned to face their pursuers on the River Aisne. This was an ideal defensive position for them as it was north of the river and on high ground which stretched for some 25 miles. The British Expeditionary Force forced their way across the river on 12 September. Unfortunately a full breakthrough was prevented and repeated Allied attacks over the next four days failed to make progress on to the high ground. Ernest was killed during this action on 14 September 1914. His death is recorded on the La Ferte-sous-Jouarre Memorial. This is located on the south bank of the River Marne, some 66 km east of Paris. It commemorates nearly 4,000 officers and men of the British Expeditionary Force who fell at either Mons, Le Cateau, on the Marne or the Aisne between August and the early part of October 1914 and who have no known grave.

His name appears on the Memorial board in St Mary's Church, Hailsham although it did not appear in the 'Roll of Honour' printed earlier in the parish magazine. Despite growing up in Hailsham and presumably being educated locally, his name does not appear on the Memorial board in Hailsham Council Boys School.

ꆂꆂꆂꆂꆂꆂꆂꆂꆂꆂ

Note – There were actually two people with the identical name of 'Ernest Alfred Pelling', who served in the Royal Sussex Regiment during WW1 and both held the rank of 'Private'.

Part Two – The Great War: 1914-18

Potter, Charles

Rank	Regiment	Age at Death
?	?	35 or 36yrs

Charles Potter was born at Eastbourne in 1881, the son of Charles and Eliza Potter. He was living in Eastbourne with his parents at the time of the census in both 1891 and 1901. In 1911, Charles, now aged 29 years, was married to Sophia Elizabeth Potter and had been for about three years although they did not have any children at that stage. He described himself as a bricklayer's labourer and they were living at Elm Cottage, Mill Road in Hailsham.

Whilst it has been possible to identify the pre-war life of Charles Potter for whom records never show a second name, it has not been so easy to ascertain details of his military service. Based purely on age, there appear to be two possibilities.

The first possibility is that he was a Bombardier in the Royal Field Artillery (*Service No: L/11867*).This 'C.H.Potter' served in the 156th Brigade, Heavy Artillery. He died on 26 July 1916 and is buried at Flatiron Copse Cemetery, in Mametz on the Somme, France. (*Grave Ref: I.C.5.*)

The second possibility is that he was a Private in the Royal Army Service Corps (*Service No: M2/078011*).This 'C.H.Potter' was in No.5 Section, Anti-Aircraft workshop. He died on 28th December 1917 and is buried at Rocquigny-Equancourt Road British Cemetery, Manacourt, on the Somme in France. (*Grave Ref: VII.D.9*)

Unfortunately both possibilities have an 'H' as a second initial and 'our' Charles Potter never shows himself in the census records with a second initial. In addition, there are thirteen other people with the name of either 'C' or 'Charles' Potter according to Commonwealth War Graves information. Each of these can, of course, be identified by either rank, Regiment or date of death.

Charles Potter's death is commemorated on the Memorial board in St Mary's Church, Hailsham, which does not show any other details. His name is not shown in the 'Roll of Honour' printed earlier in the parish magazine, nor does his name appear on the Hailsham Council Boys School Memorial board, both of which would have provided clues to his military service. It is unfortunate that the available records have not allowed a more positive identification.

ﺽﺽﺽﺽﺽﺽﺽﺽﺽﺽ

Pye, Arthur

Rank	Regiment	Age at Death
Private	London	26yrs

Arthur Pye was born in Westerham, Kent in 1891, one of the two sons of Arthur Edwin and Louisa Pye. In 1901, the family were living at 20 High Street, Hailsham. Arthur was 10 years old and his father, described as an employer, was a leather merchant and shoe seller. The Pye family are shown in the 1911 census in Hailsham where Arthur Edwin and Louisa Pye were living with their 17 year old daughter at 20 High Street, Hailsham and from where he was running his business of boot, shoe and leather seller. At the time, Arthur was boarding with a family in Southend-on-Sea and was working as an Accountant's Clerk for the Southend Waterworks Company. Arthur subsequently got married to Ethel and they had a son, Reginald. When he joined up, he gave his address as Burchetts Farm, Whitesmith, Halland.

He enlisted in the Sun Street Recruiting Office in London into the London Regiment and served as a Private (*Service No: 2696*) in the 7th Battalion. He was killed in action on the Somme on 7th October 1916, aged 26 years.

He is buried in Warlencourt British cemetery in the Pas de Calais Department of France (*Grave Ref: Plot 1.Row F. Grave 12*). The inscription says *"Until the day breaks"*.This cemetery now contains some 3,500 Commonwealth burials and commemorations of the First World War of which 1,800 of the burials are unidentified. His brother, Edwin, also served in the war but he survived.

Having been educated at Hailsham, the name and rank of *"Private A. Pye"* appears on the Hailsham Boys School 'Roll of Honour'. His name also appears in the 'Roll of Honour' printed in the parish magazine in 1918 as well as on the Memorial board in St Mary's Church, Hailsham. In addition, being an apparent member of the Weslyan congregation, he is commemorated on the Memorial tablet in Hailsham Methodist Church.

൰൰൰൰൰൰൰൰൰൰

Richardson, Henry J.

Rank	Regiment	Age at Death
Private Private	(1) Middlesex (2) London	29yrs

Henry Jesse Richardson (later known just as Jesse) was born in Hailsham in 1889, the son of William Richardson, a matting weaver,and his wife, Mercy. In 1891, the family, with Jesse, then aged 2 years were living at 17 Gordon Place, Hailsham. In 1911, Jesse was single and by then aged 22 years. The family, consisting of Jesse, his parents and now four sisters were living at 3 Palmers Row, Hailsham. Jesse was now employed as a mat maker in the matting department of Burfields, the Rope and Twine factory in Hailsham.

He was still working at Burfields when he enlisted in March 1916 at the Purfleet, Surrey Recruiting Office, into the Middlesex Regiment. He served as a Private (*Service No: 6634*) in the 7th Battalion and went to the Front in August 1916. He subsequently transferred into the London Regiment and served as a Private (*Service No: 493179*) with the 13th Battalion, (Princess Louise's Kensington Battalion). It would appear that the battalion was probably taking part in the third battle of Ypres, generally referred to as Passchendaele. The offensive started on 31 July 1917 and it quickly became apparent that it was not progressing as planned. Ceaseless rain fell during the next two weeks, which gave the Germans time to reorganise and bring up reinforcements. The next British attack took place on 16 August but little progress was made mainly because of the mud. Jesse was killed in this action on 16 August 1917, aged 29 years. He is buried in Divisional Collecting Post Cemetery & Extension, Belgium (*Grave Ref: II.H.13*).

This cemetery was begun by field ambulances in August 1917 and continued in use until January 1918. Between 1924 and 1926, the original cemetery was considerably enlarged when graves were brought in from the surrounding battlefields and some small burial grounds in the area. The Extension contains nearly 700 Commonwealth burials, of which over 500 are unidentified.

Having been brought up and educated at Hailsham, the name and rank of "*Private H.J. Richardson*" appears on the Hailsham Boys School 'Roll of Honour'. His name also appears in the 'Roll of Honour' printed in the parish magazine in 1918 as well as on the Memorial board in St Mary's Church, Hailsham. He is also shown in Burfields 'Roll of Honour' written in their day book under the heading of "*The Factory Recorder*".

֍֍֍֍֍֍֍֍֍֍

Rigglesford, Edgar

Rank	Regiment	Age at Death
Private	Royal Sussex	23yrs

Edgar Rigelsford (or Rigglesford) was born at Hailsham in 1892, the second son of George and Frances Rigelsford. In 1901, Edgar was living at 14 Ersham Road, Hailsham with his parents and an elder brother. In 1911, his father, George was employed as the local sexton and they were living at the Cemetery Lodge in Hailsham. Edgar was then aged 19 years and employed as a grocer's Assistant. He was later employed at Adam's Stores, Redhill in Surrey and shortly before the outbreak of the war became an Agent for the Royal London Insurance Office at Lewes.

In September 1914, Edgar re-joined the 5th Sussex Territorials, the Royal Sussex Regiment (in which he had already served five years) as a Private (*Service No: TF5/2604*) with the 1/5th Battalion, 1st Division. On 18 February 1915, he went out to France. Although initially reported as 'missing', it was eventually confirmed that he had been killed in action having taken part in the disastrous '*historic charge*' when the 4th & 5th battalions went '*over the top*' at Aubers Ridge, near Richebourg L'Avoue in France on 9 May 1915 and over 11,000 men were killed (*See page 110 for further details*). Edgar died that day, aged 23 years old, along with Charles Hollebon, George Smith and John Tingley.

Q.M.-Sergeant H. Roberts, a former teacher at Hailsham Boys School described how Private Rigelsford "*sacrificed himself for his wounded comrades, going over the breastworks three times under howitzer, shrapnel, maxim gun and rifle fire to fetch them in. Had he returned, he would have been recommended by Captain (now Major) Courthope for honours and no honours were ever more fully deserved than in Edgar's case*". In his Parish Letter in June 1915, Rev F. Clyde Harvey wrote: -"*..... Does not Edgar Rigelsford call from France? Three times he went back to save a wounded comrade and, on the third, he died a martyr.*"

His death is commemorated on the Le Touret Memorial in the Pas de Calais, France (*Memorial Ref: Panel 20 & 21*). His war service earned him the 1915 Star, the Victory and British war medals. Having been educated at Hailsham, the name and rank of "*Private E. Rigglesford*" appears on the Hailsham Boys School Memorial board. His name also appears on the Memorial board in St Mary's Church, Hailsham as well as in the 'Roll of Honour' printed earlier in the parish magazine.

๑๑๑๑๑๑๑๑๑๑

Part Two – The Great War: 1914-18

Rigglesford, T.E.

Rank	Regiment	Age at Death
Private	Royal Sussex	26yrs

Thomas Ernest Rigglesford was born in Hailsham in August 1888, the son of Thomas and Katherine Rigglesford. In 1891, Thomas, aged 2 years was living in South Road with his parents and two elder sisters, his father being employed as a Nursery Labourer. Ten years later, in 1901, the family were living at 57 South Road, Hailsham and Thomas is aged 12 years and still at school. In 1911, the family consisting of the parents and Thomas' younger brother and two sisters were still at 57 South Road, Hailsham. Thomas is not at the family home as he had already joined the Royal Sussex Regiment. His military papers showed that, later, his parents had moved and were then living at Waverley House, Sackville Road, Hailsham.

Thomas, who had previously been a volunteer with the 2nd Sussex, Royal Field Artillery, enlisted at Eastbourne in January 1907 at the age of 18 years 5 months into the Royal Sussex Regiment and gave his occupation as 'factory labourer'. He served as a Private (*Service No: L/8652*) in the 1st Battalion, Indian Army and went to India in September 1908. In 1911, Thomas is shown on the census in the Overseas Military section with the 1st Royal Sussex Regiment at Rawalpindi, Punjab, India. At that time he was the regimental cook.

He had several spells in the various military hospitals in India during 1915 mainly classed as bronchial or laryngitis problems. He was eventually diagnosed as suffering from Tuberculosis and eventually died of this illness in India on 26 July 1915, aged 26 years, having served over eight and a half years with the Regiment. He is buried in Murree New Cemetery, Karachi and commemorated on the Karachi War Memorial.

The Karachi War Cemetery lies a few miles from the centre of Karachi. It was created by the Commonwealth War Graves Commission to receive the graves from a number of civil and temporary military cemeteries scattered through the north of Pakistan and the tribal areas, where their permanent maintenance was not possible. One of these cemeteries since found impossible to maintain adequately was Murree New Cemetery.

As he was brought up in Hailsham, he would probably have been educated locally but for some reason his name does not appear on the Boys School Memorial board. However, it does appear on the Memorial board in St Mary's Church, Hailsham even though it did not appear in the 'Roll of Honour' printed earlier in the parish magazine.

שּׁשּׁשּׁשּׁשּׁשּׁשּׁשּׁשּׁשּׁ

Ripley, Abraham (1)

Rank	Regiment	Age at Death
Private Private	(1) Royal West Kent (2) Middlesex	23yrs

Abraham Ripley (*the first of two with this name*) was born in Hollington, Hastings in 1894, the son of Moses and Matilda Ripley. He was the nephew of the other Abraham Ripley shown on the war Memorial. In 1911, Abraham (*Abram*), then aged 17 years, was living with his parents, his four brothers and two sisters at Ripleys Cottages, Magham Down, Hailsham and was employed as a gardener.

Abraham enlisted at the Chichester Recruiting Office into the Royal West Kent Regiment and gave his residence as being Magham Down. He later transferred to the Duke of Cambridge's Own, the Middlesex Regiment where he served as a Private (*Service No: G/40970*) in the 4th Battalion, 37th Division. The regiment took part in the action later known as Passchendaele, which started on 31 July and lasted until November 1917. The Allies' initial aim was to dislodge the Germans from their dominating positions on the ridge of high ground in Belgium between Westroosbeke and Broodseinde before winter. The operation depended on speed for success since records showed that, at best, there would probably only be three weeks without rain at that time of year. The offensive was launched on 31 July 1917 in heavy mist and it was on that day that Abraham was killed in action aged 23 years. The family recall being told that he was '*shot in the mouth*'.

His body was never identified or recovered and his death is commemorated on the Menin Gate Memorial, Ypres in Belgium (*Memorial Ref: Panel 49 & 51*).

Having been brought up and educated at Hailsham, the name and rank of "*Private A. Ripley*" appears on the Hailsham Boys School Memorial board. His name also appears on the Memorial board in St Mary's Church, Hailsham as well as in the 'Roll of Honour' printed earlier in the parish magazine, where he is shown as a Private in the 4th Middlesex Regiment.

ZZZZZZZZZZ

Ripley, Abraham (2)

Rank	Regiment	Age at Death
Lance Corporal	Royal Fusiliers	29yrs

Abraham Ripley (*the second of two with this name*) was born in Hastings in November 1889, the son of Mark and Olive (nee Bird) Ripley. He was the uncle of the other Abraham Ripley shown on the war Memorial. In the 1901 census, Abraham was living with his parents and several siblings. The family have been recorded twice. The first census record shows them living in a van at Amberstone whilst the second describes them as living in a caravan in Harebeating Road. By the time he joined up, he was married to Susannah, his address was Harebeating, Hailsham and his parents were shown as living at Biggin Hill, Kent.

Abraham enlisted at Bromley in Kent, where his uncle and aunt lived. He joined the Royal Fusiliers where he served as a Private (*Service No: 5743*) in the 30th Regiment. He subsequently transferred to the Royal Fusiliers (City of London Regiment), 7th Battalion (*Service No: 51313*) and rose to become a Lance Corporal. The area near Cambrai and the Hindenburg Line was fought over for nearly the duration of the war and the battlefield sites seen today reflect that. The Allies were convinced that the Line could now be broken by combining all Allied armies in the west in simultaneous offensives. On 27 September 1918, Haig's army thrust against the Hindenburg Line. As part of this, the Royal Fusiliers were in action near Bourlon Wood and their objective was to capture the spur running south west of this. Abraham was killed in this action by "*shell-fire*" on 29 September 1918, aged 29 years.

He is buried in Quarry Wood Cemetery, Sains-Les-Marquion, in the Pas de Calais Department of France (*Grave Ref: II.B.23*). His war service earned him both the British and Victory medals.

Having been brought up and educated at Hailsham, the name and rank of "*Corporal A. Ripley*" appears on the Hailsham Boys School Memorial board. His name also appears on the Memorial board in St Mary's Church, Hailsham as well as in the 'Roll of Honour' printed earlier in the parish magazine, where he is shown as a Corporal in the Royal Fusiliers.

நாநாநாநாநாநாநாநாநாநா

Part Two – The Great War: 1914-18

Ripley, George

Rank	Regiment	Age at Death
Private	Queen's (Royal West Surrey)	22yrs

George Ripley was born at Brighton around 1895, the son of George and Nancy Ripley. George is the cousin of Abraham (2) Ripley. The family travelled around the countryside and, in 1901, George is shown as aged 6 years with two sisters and four brothers living with their parents in a caravan at Hollington, St Leonards. The family moved to Hailsham at some time and George went to school there for a while. In 1911, the census shows that they had moved again and were then living at 241 Old Lane, Hollington, Hastings.

His military service is slightly uncertain because Commonwealth War Grave information shows two persons named 'George Ripley' and both are Privates. It is most likely that 'our' George Ripley is the one who enlisted at Chichester into the Queen's (Royal West Surrey) Regiment as military records show him, or rather his next-of-kin, as residing in Northiam, in Sussex which is in the area in which he had been living. George served as a Private (*Service No G/14223*) with the 8th Battalion, which apparently took part in the 3rd battle of Ypres, later just known as Passchendaele. The initial aim was to dislodge the Germans from their dominating positions on the ridge of high ground in Belgium between Westroosbeke and Broodseinde before winter. Speed was essential because of the possibility of heavy rain within a few weeks. The offensive started on 31 July 1917 and it soon became apparent that that attack was not progressing as planned. Very soon the ceaseless rain brought the advance to an end with the infantry sinking up to their thighs in mud. George was badly wounded during this 3rd Battle of Ypres and tragically died of his wounds on 2nd August 1917. He was buried at Poperinghe New Military Cemetery, West Vlaanderen in Belgium (*Grave Ref: II.C.39*).

Having been educated at Hailsham, the name and rank of "*Private G. Ripley*" appears on the Hailsham Boys School Memorial board and also on the Memorial board in St Mary's Church, Hailsham. His name does not appear in the 'Roll of Honour' printed earlier in the parish magazine which would then have provided conclusive evidence of the Regiment in which he served. His death is also recorded on the Northiam War Memorial.

༒༒༒༒༒༒༒༒༒༒

Part Two – The Great War: 1914-18

Saunders, Charles

Rank	Regiment	Age at Death
Private	Royal Fusiliers	38yrs

Charles Saunders was born in Hailsham in 1878, the eldest son of Thomas and Caroline Saunders. In 1901, the family were living at White Dyke, Hailsham. Charles, aged 23 years, was employed as an agricultural labourer and living with his parents, one sister and two younger brothers, one of whom was Ernest Saunders who died almost a year after Charles was killed. In 1911, Charles, then aged 33 years, was single and living with his parents, this time at Northeath Farm, Harebeating, Hailsham. He was employed as a farm labourer.

He was still resident in Hailsham when he enlisted at the Eastbourne Recruiting Office into the Royal Fusiliers (City of London Regiment). He served as a Private (*Service No: 27156*) with the 9th Battalion, 12th Division. This Battalion went to France and Flanders in May 1915. Charles was in action on the Somme Battle Front during, what is now referred to as, the War of Attrition. This lasted from mid July until the end of November 1916. During this time, the Allies had only advanced just over eight miles along a twenty mile front with the loss of some 420,000 British and 195,000 French troops. At the same time, the Germans had lost some 650,000 troops. Charles was killed in that action on 7th October 1916. His death is commemorated on the Thiepval Memorial (*Memorial Ref: Pier and Face 8C, 9A & 16A*)

Having been brought up and educated at Hailsham, the name and rank of "*Private C. Saunders*" appears on the Hailsham Boys School Memorial board. His name also appears on the Memorial board in St Mary's Church and the 'Roll of Honour' printed earlier in the parish magazine.

ꙎꙎꙎꙎꙎꙎꙎꙎꙎꙎ

Saunders, Ernest

Rank	Regiment	Age at Death
Private Private	(1) Royal Army Service Corps (2) Suffolk	31yrs

Ernest S. Saunders was born in Hailsham in 1886, the youngest son of Thomas and Caroline Saunders. In 1901, the family were living at White Dyke, Hailsham. Ernest, aged 15 years, was employed as a carter on a farm and was living with his parents, one sister and two older brothers, one of whom was Charles Saunders who was killed in action almost a year before Ernest was to die. By 1911, Ernest, aged 25 years had left home and was married to Elizabeth Smith (*sister of George Smith who is one of those named on the Memorial*). At that time they had one son aged 1½ years and were living at "Compton", Sackville Road, Hailsham. Ernest was then employed as a farm labourer. Before he joined up, the family had increased to six children, they had moved to Ginger's Green Cottage at Herstmonceux and George was working as a milkman for Mr W. Barrow, at Sackville Farm.

He enlisted at the Aldershot Recruiting Office into the Royal Army Service Corps, Motor Transport (*Service No: T4/172802*). He subsequently transferred to the Suffolk Regiment where he served as a Private (*Service No: 50631*) with the 2nd Battalion. He was wounded in the knee and suffered shell shock probably during the Battle of Arras and Vimy Ridge. After he was wounded, Elizabeth had an urgent message to go to France to see him at the base hospital at Etaples. Although she arrived in time, George died of his wounds on 22nd May 1917. The area around Etaples was the scene of immense concentrations of Commonwealth reinforcement camps and hospitals. It was remote from attack, except from aircraft, and accessible by railway from the main battlefields. In 1917, 100,000 troops were camped among the sand dunes and the hospitals. Ernest is buried in Etaples Military Cemetery, in the Pas de Calais Department of France (*Grave Ref: XXV.D.17A – original grave no. 163*). When Elizabeth returned to England, she found herself and the six children evicted from the tied cottage at Gingers Green where they then lived as the farmer wanted to employ another farm hand.

Having been brought up and educated in Hailsham, the name and rank of "*Private E. Saunders*" appears on the Hailsham Boys School Memorial board. His name also appears on the Memorial board in St Mary's Church, Hailsham as well as in the 'Roll of Honour' printed earlier in the parish magazine.

೮೮೮೮೮೮೮೮೮೮

Part Two – The Great War: 1914-18

Saunders, John, MM

Rank	Regiment	Age at Death
Sergeant	Royal Horse Artillery	29yrs

John Saunders was born at Hailsham in 1889, the son of William and Fanny Saunders. In 1901, John, aged 11 years was living with his family at 32 Battle Road, Hailsham with his parents, two older and two younger brothers. In 1911, his parents were still living in Battle Road, Hailsham but John and his two elder brothers had left home.

According to the "*Sussex Daily News*" in December 1916, John was the third of the four sons of Mr and Mrs William Saunders who were serving their country and also that Bombardier John Saunders had been in the army for eight years, having been called from India to take part in the war. Anyway, John re-enlisted in September 1914 at the Eastbourne Recruiting Office into the Royal Horse Artillery and went to France in 1915. He later took part in the landing on the Gallipoli Peninsular before going to Salonika, Egypt where he served (*Service No: 52182*) with "B" Battery, 15th Brigade. He then went to Serbia where he gained the Serbian Gold Medal. He rose to become a Sergeant. He was wounded in action and died of his wounds in the base hospital at Rouen, France on 20 October 1917. He is buried in St Sever Cemetery Extension at Rouen (*Grave Ref: P.III.O.1B*). His war service also earned him the 1915 Star, the Victory and British war medals, in addition to the Military Medal.

The Military Medal was established by King George V in March 1916 to be awarded on the recommendation of a Commander-in-Chief in the field for "a*cts of gallantry and devotion to duty performed by non-commissioned officers and men of our army in the field*". Such award was announced officially in the London Gazette but just as a list of names without the citation. John was awarded the Military Medal whilst he was still a Lance-Corporal for good work during operations at the Canal du Nord. The medal recommendation was reported in the Parish magazine and says: - "*His conduct was extremely courageous throughout and fine work for so young a soldier*". It was owing to his work in Serbia that he was also awarded "The Serbian Gold Medal" but no details of this award have yet been traced.

Having been brought up and educated at Hailsham, the name and rank of "*Sergeant J. Saunders, MM*" appears on the Hailsham Boys School Memorial board. His name also appears on the Memorial board in St Mary's Church, Hailsham. The 'Roll of Honour' printed in the parish magazine also gives his rank: "*Sergeant, Royal Horse Artillery*" and shows his award of both the Military Medal and also the Serbian Gold Medal.

ꙮ ꙮ ꙮ ꙮ ꙮ ꙮ ꙮ ꙮ ꙮ ꙮ

Part Two – The Great War: 1914-18

Seamer, Frederick J.

Rank	Regiment	Age at Death
Gunner Private	(1) Royal Field Artillery (2) Coldstream Guards	?

Frederick Charles Seamer was born at Seaford in 1896, the eldest of the three sons of Charles Seamer, a bricklayer. Sometime around 1900, Frederick's mother died and his father was left a widower with the three children. In 1901, Frederick, aged 5 years, was living at 52 High Street, Hailsham with his father and the youngest brother, together with a housekeeper and three young men as boarders. The second son had been taken to live at Pale House Common, near Framfield with his grandparents. Frederick continued to live in Hailsham which is where he was educated. Ten years later, in 1911, Frederick, aged 15 years, is still living with his father and youngest brother and a servant/housekeeper. He is shown as being a carpenter's apprentice.

Frederick was a big lad for his age and was obviously very keen on joining the army. On 24 January 1913, when he was just 16 years old, he enlisted into the Royal Field Artillery at "The Laurels" in North Street which was the Hailsham Recruiting Office. He put himself forward as being 19 years old and this age was accepted. His enlistment papers showed his height at 5ft 7¾ ins and chest size of 36¾ ins. He had used his real name and gave the correct address for his father. The family already had an inkling that he might try to join up and the housekeeper had hidden his boots to prevent this happening. Unfortunately, this ruse failed and the next time they saw him, he was proudly marching down the road behind the Recruiting Sergeant wearing his school football boots!

He enlisted initially as a Gunner (*Service No: 613*) with the Royal Field Artillery, as shown by his Attestation papers but all of his remaining military records were lost in a warehouse fire in London in WW2 following a bombing raid. Frederick apparently transferred into the Coldstream Guards where he served as a Private. Despite his name being on the Hailsham Boys School Memorial board, which means that he been killed prior to August 1919, no details of his actual date of death nor the action in which he was killed, have yet been traced.

Having been educated at Hailsham, the name and rank of "*Private F.J. Seamer*" appears on the Hailsham Boys School Memorial board. His name also appears on the Memorial board in St Mary's Church, Hailsham. It also appears in the 'Roll of Honour' printed earlier in the parish magazine, which showed him as being a Private in the Coldstream Guards. All three of these records show his initials as being "F.J." Seamer whereas his proper name was, apparently, Frederick Charles Seamer.

෴෴෴෴෴෴෴෴෴

Part Two – The Great War: 1914-18

Shaw, Edward L.

Rank	Regiment	Age at Death
Corporal 2nd Lieutenant	(1) Hon Royal Artillery Company (2) Royal West Surrey (Queen's)	26yrs

Edward Lockhart Shaw was born in China in 1890. The Commonwealth War Graves Commission (CWGC) records show that Edward Shaw is the son of Charles and Esther Shaw of Ireland. In 1901, Edward, aged 11 years, is a boarder along with his elder brother at the Church Missionary Children's Home in Limpsfield, Godstone in Surrey. This establishment was the home and school for the children of missionaries working under the Church Missionary Society and was initially built in 1887 for 120 children. The census return shows that Edward had been born in China but was a British Subject. No trace was found of the whereabouts of either him or his parents in the 1911 census. However the CWGC records also show that he was the husband of Gwendoline Shaw of 1124 N. Stoneham Avenue, Los Angeles, California USA which would explain why his name does not show up in the 1911 census.

He initially joined the Hon Royal Artillery Company where he rose to the rank of Corporal (*Service No: R/13196*). He subsequently gained a commission and served as a Second Lieutenant in the 9th Battalion of the Queen's, Royal West Surrey Regiment. He was killed in action and died on 5th August 1916, aged 26 years and is buried in Aveluy Communal Cemetery Extension (*Grave Ref: H.24*). Aveluy is a village in the Department of the Somme, immediately north of Albert. The Commonwealth forces held Aveluy village from July 1915 until March 1918 when the village and the cemetery were lost during the German advance. However, they were retaken at the end of August. This cemetery contains 613 burials and commemorations of the First World War. His war service earned him both the British and Victory medals, which were sent to his widow in America.

When he joined the army, it appears that he might have 'mis-represented' his age. The military records record him as being 29 years old when he was killed but the census shows that he was probably only 26 years old. His death is commemorated on the Memorial board in St Mary's Church, Hailsham and his name appears in the 'Roll of Honour' printed earlier in the parish magazine which shows him as "*2nd Lieutenant Edward Lockhart Shaw, Queens Royal West Surrey Regiment*".

Ꙩ Ꙩ Ꙩ Ꙩ Ꙩ Ꙩ Ꙩ Ꙩ Ꙩ Ꙩ

Part Two – The Great War: 1914-18

Smith, Frank C.

Rank	Regiment	Age at Death
Private	Royal Army Service Corps	24yrs

Frank Charles Smith was born at Hailsham in 1891, the son of Sidney and Maria Smith of Hailsham. In 1891, Frank was 3 months old, living at Magham Down, Hailsham with parents, Sidney, a harness maker, Maria his wife and his brother and sister. By 1901, the family had moved to 3 Station Road, Hailsham and Frank, aged 10 years was still at school although his elder brother was employed as a carpenter. In 1911, Frank's father had remarried and Frank then aged 20 years had moved and was living with his uncle & aunt, William & Emma Warman at 24 Lansdowne Gardens, London SW. Frank was employed as a clerk in the Civil Service,

He was still working as a clerk when he enlisted into the Royal Army Service Corps. He served as a Private (*Service No: T/649*) with the Home Counties Division. He was wounded in action and returned to England to convalesce. Unfortunately, he died of his wounds whilst at the Southern Hospital, Dartford on 11th September 1915 aged 24 years.

His body was brought back to Hailsham where he was buried in the Cemetery in the same grave as his mother. (*Grave space 1377*)

For some reason, his name does not appear on the Memorial board at Hailsham Boys School although he must have been educated locally. However, it does appear on the Memorial board in St Mary's Church, Hailsham even though it did not appear in the 'Roll of Honour' printed earlier in the parish Magazine.

ധധധധധധധധധ

Part Two – The Great War: 1914-18

Smith, George

Rank	Regiment	Age at Death
Private	Royal Sussex	18yrs

George Smith was born in Chiddingly in 1897, the son of Robert and Eliza Smith. In 1901, the family were living in Lower Road, Herstmonceux. George was shown as aged 4 years and his father was employed as an agricultural labourer, In 1911, George then aged 14 years, was living with his parents together with his four brothers and two sisters at Carters Corner, Hailsham. George was employed as a 'carter boy' on a farm. His sister, Elizabeth, later married Ernest Saunders who is also named on the Memorial.

George enlisted at the Hailsham Recruiting Office into the Royal Sussex Regiment. He served as a Private (*Service No: S/2146*) with the 2nd Battalion, 1st Division. He was a Reservist but took part in the '*Historic Charge*' on 9th May 1915 at the Battle of Aubers Ridge when the British troops went 'over the top' after a disastrous artillery bombardment and were cut down by machine gun fire (*See page 110 for further details*). George Smith was killed in action and was just one of over 11,000 men who were lost on that one day at Richebourg L'Avoue, in France. This was in the same action in which his fellow Hailsham comrades, Charles Hollebon, Edgar Riggelsford and John Tingley also lost their lives.

George's death is commemorated on the Le Touret Memorial which is one of those erected to record the names of the officers and men who fell in the Great War and whose graves are not known (*Memorial Ref: Panel 20 & 21*).

In February 1915, George sent a letter to his sister, Elizabeth, which said that, if he should get killed, every penny of his would go to her. This 'testamentary expression' was recognised as valid within the meaning of the Wills Act, 1837 and certified by the War Office in December 1915.

Having been brought up and educated at Hailsham, the name and rank of "*Private G. Smith*" appears on the Hailsham Boys School Memorial board. His name also appears on the Memorial board in St Mary's Church, Hailsham as well as in the 'Roll of Honour' printed earlier in the parish magazine.

ഇ ഇ ഇ ഇ ഇ ഇ ഇ ഇ ഇ ഇ

Part Two – The Great War: 1914-18

Smith, John

Rank	Regiment	Age at Death
Private Private	(1) Royal Field Artillery (2) Duke of Cornwall's Light Infantry	25yrs

John Smith was born in Hailsham around 1892, the son of John and Emma Smith. In 1901, John aged 9 years was living in the family home in Bellbanks Road in Hailsham with five siblings. Ten years later, John, then aged 19 years, single, was living with his parents John, a rope maker, and Emma his wife, together with his two brothers and one sister at "Archery Cottage", 34 Bellbanks Road in Hailsham. John was employed as a house painter. One of John's brothers was Thomas Henry Smith who died as a result of his war wounds about two years after John was killed. John and Emma Smith subsequently moved to 3 Cobden Place, Station Road in Hailsham.

John enlisted at the Eastbourne Recruiting Office firstly into the Royal Field Artillery where he served as a Private (*Service No: 148760*). He was later transferred into the Duke of Cornwall's Light Infantry also as a Private (*Service No: 28191*) in the 6th Battalion, 14th Light Division. The battalion apparently took part in, what was later referred to as, the War of Attrition. This battle started in mid July 1916 and petered out in mid November 1916. During that time, the Allies had advanced a little over eight miles on a twenty mile front. For these gains, the British lost some 420,000 troops and the French 195,000 troops whilst the Germans lost some 650,000 troops. John Smith was killed in action during this action on the Somme on 16 September 1916, aged 25 years. His death is commemorated on the Thiepval Memorial (*Memorial Ref: Pier and Face 6B*).

John is also commemorated on the memorial in Hailsham Cemetery (*Grave Space: 1189*) to his brothers, Charles Caleb Smith who died before the war in 1911 aged 17 years and Thomas Smith who died in the war, two years after John, in 1918.

Having been brought up and educated at Hailsham, the name and rank of "*Private J. Smith*" also appears on the Hailsham Boys School Memorial board. His name also appears on the Memorial board in St Mary's Church, Hailsham as well as in the 'Roll of Honour' printed earlier in the parish magazine.

ഇഇഇഇഇഇഇഇഇ

Part Two – The Great War: 1914-18

Smith, Samuel

Rank	Regiment	Age at Death
Gunner	Royal Field Artillery	37yrs

Samuel Smith was born in February 1881, the son of Samson Smith, a master carpenter and his wife, Ruth. In 1881, Samuel aged 2 months is at home with five older siblings in Union (now Hawks) Road, Hailsham. In 1891, they have moved to Victoria Road, most of the children have left home and his father is now described as a fish hawker. Tragedy subsequently struck the family as Samuel's father died and his mother remarried. In 1901, Samuel, now stepson to George Fox was aged 20 years and a twine maker in a local rope factory.

In January 1903, Samuel enlisted at Eastbourne into the Royal Horse/Field Artillery where he served as a gunner (*Service No: 30098*) in No. 1 depot. He signed on for 12 years, the first 3 years in the army and the next 9 years on the reserves. On enlistment, he was recorded as 5ft 6ins tall and he gave his occupation as a gardener. After basic training, he was posted to South Africa where he stayed for just over two years. In February 1906, on the termination of his initial 3 years, he was discharged and transferred onto the 1st class army reserve.

In 1911, Samuel, aged 30 years and now working as a butcher, was living with his mother, step-father and elder brother at 17 Garfield Road, Hailsham. In August 1911, he married Rhoda Stephens(?), a spinster from Hellingly, and they set up home at Muddles Green, Chiddingly. In August 1914, 8½ years out of his 9 years on reserve, hostilities started and Samuel was called up. By then, he and his wife had two young children and they were extremely unhappy about him being 'called up'. He was posted to France and he apparently refused to go. As a result, he was tried by Courts Martial on 30th December 1914 and sentenced to six months imprisonment. This was commuted to three months but this order was never received by the prison governor. He was only released on 13 June 1915 after his six month term and sent to rejoin his unit. His army service was terminated at the completion of his 12 years. He returned to England for discharge in January 1916. He died at Stone Cross on 24 July 1918, aged 37 years, leaving a widow and three children. This was on the same day that his step-father committed suicide *"whilst of unsound mind due to changes of old age"*. Samuel was described as a 'time expired' soldier who had spent two years in the present war. He was buried in Hailsham Cemetery along with his step-father (*Grave space: 488 – No headstone*).

Having been brought up and educated in Hailsham, the name and rank of *"Private S. Smith"* appears on the Hailsham Council Boys School Memorial board and also on the Memorial board in St Mary's Church, Hailsham. The Roll of Honour printed earlier in parish magazine, shows him (*incorrectly*) as a Private in the Royal Sussex Regiment.

ഇഇഇഇഇഇഇഇഇഇ

Part Two – The Great War: 1914-18

Smith, Thomas H.

Rank	Regiment	Age at Death
Private Private	(1) Middlesex (2) Labour Corps	20yrs

Thomas Henry Smith was born at Hailsham in 1899, the third son of John and Emma Smith. In 1901. Thomas aged 2 years was living in the family home at Bellbanks in Hailsham with five siblings. Ten yeas later, Thomas, then aged 12 years and still at school, was living with his parents, John, a rope maker, with Emma his wife, his two brothers and one sister at Archery Cottage, 34 Bellbanks Road, Hailsham. One of his brothers was John Smith who was killed in the war about two years before Thomas was to die. Before Thomas joined the army, he was working at Messrs. Knights' Nurseries, of Hailsham. He also belonged to Hailsham Brass Band and was in the Hailsham Platoon of Volunteers.

Thomas enlisted in March 1917 into the Middlesex regiment (*Service No: 82980*) and was, for a time, attached to the Army Service Corps. He subsequently transferred to the Labour Corps (*Service No: 153300*) and was working at Sutton, in Surrey when he was taken ill. He died from pneumonia following influenza at Horton War Hospital in Epsom on 2 November 1918, aged 20 years. He is buried in Hailsham Cemetery in the same grave as his brother, Charles Caleb Smith, who died before the war in 1911 aged 17 years (*Grave space: 1189*).

The Labour Corps had been formed in February 1917 and, is generally regarded as a predecessor of the Royal Pioneer Corps. At the start of WWI, the British had no organised Labour system and depended on civilians supplied by the French Government. As the war progressed demands for Labour increased, as armies grew in size and at the same time less Frenchmen were available to assist. The British started to send labourers to France in 1915-1916 to work in docks etc. In April 1917 they were formed into a Labour Corps which eventually included 325,000 British soldiers and 300,000 Prisoners of War mainly serving in France in Nov 1918.

Having been brought up and educated at Hailsham, the name and rank of "*Private T. Smith*" also appears on the Hailsham Boys School Memorial board. His name also appears on the Memorial board in St Mary's Church, Hailsham. In the 'Roll of Honour' printed earlier in the parish magazine he is shown as "*Tom Smith, Private A.S.C.*" (*Army Service Corps/Labour Corps*)

෨෨෨෨෨෨෨෨෨෨

Stickland, Alfred A.

Rank	Regiment	Age at Death
Private	Royal Sussex	37yrs

Alfred Augustus Stickland was born in Lewes around 1881, the son of Henry and Martha Stickland. In 1891, Alfred then aged 10 years was living with his parents, Henry, a coach painter, and Martha his wife, together with his two elder brothers at 4 Elim Place, Hailsham. Twenty years later, in 1911, Alfred then aged 30 years, single, was living with his father and one brother at 9 Elmsdown Place, Hailsham. His occupation was given as a butcher.

He enlisted at Eastbourne Recruiting Office into the Royal Sussex Regiment and served as a Private (*Service No: G/15975*) in the 13th Battalion, 39th Division as part of the British Expeditionary Force. The battalion appears to have taken part in the 3rd Battle of Ypres, later referred to as Passchendaele. The initial objective of this operation was to dislodge the Germans from their dominating positions on a ridge of high ground in Belgium between Westroosbeke and Broodseinde before winter. The operation depended on speed because of the threat of heavy rain within a few weeks. The downpour was both early and continuous. Ceaseless rain brought further advance to an end with infantry sinking up to their thighs in the mud. Alfred was seriously wounded during this action and tragically died of his wounds on 24 October 1917 aged 37 years. He is buried in Godeswaervelde (*Referred to be the British Tommy as "Gertie wears velvet"*) British Cemetery in a village near the Belgium border in northern France, which contains 972 Commonwealth burials from WWI (*Grave Ref: I.K.23*).

Having been brought up and educated in Hailsham, the name and rank of "*Private A.A. Stickland*" appears on the Hailsham Boys School Memorial board. His name also appears on the Memorial board in St Mary's Church, Hailsham and in the 'Roll of Honour' printed earlier in the parish magazine.

Alfred's death is also commemorated on his parent's grave in Hailsham Cemetery (*Grave No 1142*).

ധധധധധധധധധ

Tingley, John H.

Rank	Regiment	Age at Death
Private Rifleman	(1) Royal Sussex (2) Rifle Brigade	19yrs

John Henry Tingley (always known as Jack) was born in Brighton around 1896, the son of Henry and Georgina Tingley. In 1911, Jack then aged 15 years, was living with his parents, Henry, a policeman, and Georgina his wife together with his three sisters at 'Batchelors Bump', Fairlight, near Hastings. Jack was then employed as a milk boy (domestic). His parents moved to 3 Western Road, Hailsham in 1913 when his father, P.C. Tingley, transferred to the Police Station in Hailsham.

In February 1913, Jack enlisted at the Chichester Recruiting Office into the Royal Sussex Regiment (*Service No: G/1869*). Just prior to the beginning of the war, he transferred to the Rifle Brigade (The Prince Consort's Own) where he served as a Rifleman (*Service No: 5531*) with the 2nd Battalion, 8th Division. He went to the Front a few weeks after the commencement of the war and saw action in France and Flanders. He was invalided home with frost-bitten feet in December 1914. He recovered and went back to the Front in March 1915. He wrote home regularly until early May 1915. His parents received no more letters from him but heard from his comrades that he had been killed. They finally received confirmation that he was killed in action on 9 May

1915 aged 19 years. He was another who had taken part in the disastrous '*historic charge*' when the 4th & 5th battalions went '*over the top*' at Aubers Ridge, near Richebourg L'Avoue in France and over 11,000 men were killed (*See page 110 for further details*). In the same action, his fellow Hailsham comrades Charles Hollebon, George Smith and Edgar Rigglesford were also killed.

His death is commemorated on the Ploegsteert Memorial, which stands in Berks Cemetery extension, some 12 kms south of Ypres in Belgium (*Memorial Ref: Panel 10*). This memorial commemorates more than 11,000 servicemen of the United Kingdom and South African forces who died in this sector during WWI and have no known grave.

His name appears on the Memorial board in St Mary's Church, Hailsham as well as in the 'Roll of Honour' printed earlier in the parish magazine.

Jack's death is also commemorated on his parent's grave in Hailsham Cemetery (*Grave Space No 3098*).

ಗಗಗಗಗಗಗಗಗಗ

Toye, Claude L.

Rank	Regiment	Age at Death
Lance Corporal	Royal Sussex	27yrs

Claude Leonard Toye was born in Haywards Heath in 1889, the son of Alfred and Rosamund Toye. In 1891, Claude then aged 2 years was living in Cuckfield with his parents, Alfred, an Asylum Attendant, and Rosamund his wife together with his five brothers and two sisters. In 1911, Claude then aged 22 years, still single, was assisting in his brother's china, glass & hardware business and was living with his married brother, Clement Toye, and sister-in-law, at 13 Station Road, Hailsham.

Claude enlisted at the Bexhill Recruiting Office into the Royal Sussex Regiment (*Service No: SD/3034*) and served in the 13th battalion, 39th Division as part of the British Expeditionary Force. He was killed in action on the Rue de Bois on 30 June 1916, aged 27 years. The action in which he lost his life was the Battle of Boar's Head and Claude was the third Hailsham man to die, along with Nelson Carter and David Parsons (*Refer to pages 150 – 152 for further details of this action*). This battle was the diversionary attack when Lowther's Lambs went '*over the top*'. This battle was designed, but disastrously failed, to distract attention from the major offensive on the Somme due to start the following day.

Claude is buried in Cabaret Rouge British cemetery in the Pas de Calais, France (*Grave Ref: XV.N.29*). This cemetery now contains 7,655 Commonwealth burials of the First World War, more than half of them being unidentified.

His death is commemorated on the Haywards Heath, Hastings and Hailsham War Memorials as well as in Blacklands Parish Church in Hastings. His name also appears on the Memorial board in St Mary's Church, Hailsham as well as in the 'Roll of Honour' printed earlier in the parish magazine.

಩಩಩಩಩಩಩಩಩಩಩

Part Two – The Great War: 1914-18

Vine, Bert

Rank	Regiment	Age at Death
Private	Royal Sussex	25yrs

Bert Vine was born in Hailsham in 1893, the son of Matthew and Caroline Vine. In 1901, Bertie aged 8 years was living in the family home at 4 Palmers Row in Hailsham with five siblings. Ten years later, Bert, then aged 18 years, was still at home living with his parents, Matthew, a hemp dresser, and Caroline his wife together with his two brothers at Mountview Terrace, Sackville Road, Hailsham. Bert was then employed as a string maker at Burfield's Rope and Twine factory in South Road, Hailsham.

Bert was still employed at Burfield's in the twine department when he enlisted at the Chichester recruiting Office into the Royal Sussex Regiment. He served as a Private (*Service No: TF/202989*) in the 1/5th Battalion as part of the British Expeditionary Force. In July 1915, Bert's parents had the distinction of having five sons and four sons-in-law serving their King and Country in the Army with one son doing his bit on Government contract work in Croydon. Unfortunately, Bert was killed in action on 12 October 1917, aged 25 years. He is buried in Vlamertinghe New Military Cemetery, Belgium (*Plot IX .F. 27*).

This cemetery is located near Ieper, West-Vlaanderen. For much of the First World War, Vlamertinghe (now Vlamertinge) was just outside the normal range of German shell-fire and the village was used both by artillery units and field ambulances. Burials were made in the original Military Cemetery until June 1917, when the New Military Cemetery was begun in anticipation of the Allied offensive launched on this part of the front in July. Although the cemetery continued in use until October 1918, most of the burials are from July to December 1917 and it now contains just over 1,800 Commonwealth burials of the First World War.

Having been brought up and educated in Hailsham, the name and rank of "*Private E. Vine*" appears on the Hailsham Boys School Memorial board. His name also appears on the Memorial board in St Mary's Church, Hailsham as well as in the 'Roll of Honour' printed earlier in the parish magazine. Being an employee of Burfield's, his name appears in the 'Roll of Honour' in their Factory Record and Visitors book under the heading "*The Factory Recorder*".

൰൰൰൰൰൰൰൰൰൰

Part Two – The Great War: 1914-18

Vine, James Uriah

Rank	Regiment	Age at Death
Gunner	Royal Horse/Field Artillery	37yrs

James Uriah Vine was born in Hailsham in 1881, the son of George and Ellen Vine. In 1891, James aged 10 years was living near Albert Place, Hailsham with his parents, George who was a clerk in the Twine Factory, Ellen his wife together with his two brothers and two sisters. In 1901, James, at age 20 years, had left the family home at 5 South Road, Hailsham and was living in South Street, Worthing where he was employed as a draper's assistant. In 1911, James, then aged 30 years and still single, had moved again and was living at 20 Denne Parade, Horsham. His occupation was shown as being an assistant in a Drapers (Drapery warehouse). He later married, moved back to Hailsham as he is described as being the husband of Mrs A. C. Emily Vine of "Llanberis", 53 Summerheath Road, Hailsham. His parents were then living at Glenthorne, Ersham Road, Hailsham.

James enlisted at the Eastbourne Recruiting Office into the Royal Horse and Field Artillery and served as a Gunner (*Service No: 212574*) in C Battery, 110th Brigade in France and Flanders. He died in action on 23rd January 1918, aged 37 years and is buried in Grevillers British Cemetery in the Pas de Calais, France (*Grave Ref: X.D.7*).

The village of Grevillers was first occupied by Commonwealth troops in March 1917 and in April and May, the Australian Casualty Clearing Stations were posted nearby. They began the cemetery and continued to use it until March 1918, when Grevillers was lost to the Germans during their great advance. In August 1918, the New Zealand Division recaptured Grevillers and the Cemetery was brought into use again.

After his death, his widow expressed her thanks, through St Mary's parish magazine, to all her friends who had sent her their best wishes in her sad bereavement.

His name does not appear on the Hailsham Boys School Memorial board. However it does appear on the Memorial board in St Mary's Church, Hailsham and also in the 'Roll of Honour' printed earlier in the parish magazine.

೮೮೮೮೮೮೮೮೮೮

Walker, Arthur

Rank	Regiment	Age at Death
Private	Royal Sussex	22yrs

Arthur Richard Walker was born at Hailsham in 1895, the son of William and Elizabeth Walker. In 1901, Arthur was aged 6 years was living with his family at White Dyke, Hailsham. In 1911, Arthur, aged 16 years, was shown as being a farmer's son working on the farm and living with his parents, one brother and one sister still at White Dyke, Hailsham.

Arthur enlisted at the Eastbourne Recruiting Office into the Royal Sussex Regiment. Their records appear to show that he was born at Polegate but Hailsham is the most likely as this is shown on both 1901 and 1911 census returns. He served as a Private (*Service No: SD/3812*) with the 12th Battalion, 39th Division as part of the British Expeditionary Force. The battalion took part in the 3rd battle of Ypres, later referred to as Passchendaele. The initial objective of this operation was to dislodge the Germans from their dominating positions on a ridge of high ground in Belgium between Westroosbeke and Broodseinde before winter. The operation depended on speed because of the threat of heavy rain within a few weeks. The downpour was both early and continuous. Ceaseless rain brought further advance to an end, with infantry sinking up to their thighs in the mud. Arthur was seriously wounded in this action on the Somme and tragically died of his wounds on 8th September 1917.

He is buried in Larch Wood (Railway Cutting) Military Cemetery in Belgium (*Grave Ref: IV. G.7*). This cemetery was started in April 1915 and remained in use until April 1918 when the Western Front had moved away from the area.

Having been brought up and educated in Hailsham, the name and rank of "*Private A. Walker*" appears on the Hailsham Boys School Memorial board. His name also appears on the Memorial board in St Mary's Church, Hailsham as well as in the 'Roll of Honour' printed earlier in the parish magazine.

ཀྐཀྐཀྐཀྐཀྐཀྐ

Part Two – The Great War: 1914-18

Walker, Percy E.

Rank	Regiment	Age at Death
Private	Royal Sussex	27yrs

Percy Edward Walker was born at Eastbourne in 1889, the son of Jonathan and Mary Walker. In 1891, Percy, then aged 2 years was living at Otham Drove, Polegate, with his parents, Jonathan, a bath chairman, Mary his wife, two brothers and three sisters. In 1901, Percy aged 12 years was living in the family home in Sackville Road, Hailsham with three siblings. His mother had presumably died and his father had remarried as his wife's name is now Lucy. Ten years later, Percy, then aged 22 years and single, was living with his widowed aunt at 15 Garfield Road, Hailsham. His occupation was given as a farm labourer.

Percy enlisted at the Eastbourne Recruiting Office in September 1914 into the Royal Sussex Regiment and gave his occupation as a gardener. He also stated that he was single and that his parents were living at Sandrocks Cottages, Hailsham. He served as a Private (*Service No: SD/255*) with the 11th Battalion, 39th Division. He was killed in action on the Somme on 8th October 1916, aged 27 years. He was buried in Auchonvillers (*Usually referred to as 'Ocean Villas' by the British Tommy*) Military Cemetery, on the Somme, France (*Grave Ref: II.G.28*). He posthumously received the British War and Victory medals for his war service.

Until the summer of 1915, this part of the front was held by French troops, who began the military cemetery. It continued in use by Commonwealth field ambulances and fighting units but burials practically ceased with the German withdrawal in February 1917. The French graves were later removed leaving a total of 528 Commonwealth burials.

Percy Walker's death is commemorated on both the Eastbourne and Hailsham War Memorials and also in Christchurch Parish Church, Hampshire.

Having been brought up and educated in Hailsham, the name and rank of "*Private P.E. Walker*" appears on the Hailsham Boys School Memorial board. His name also appears on the Memorial board in St Mary's Church, Hailsham as well as in the 'Roll of Honour' printed earlier in the parish magazine.

டௌௌௌௌௌௌௌௌௌௌ

Part Two – The Great War: 1914-18

Willard, Albert E.

Rank	Regiment	Age at Death
Lieutenant	Royal Sussex	25yrs

Albert Ellis Willard was born at East Hoathly in 1893, the eldest son of Albert and Mary Willard. In 1911, Albert, then aged 18 years and single, was living at the "Court House", Hailsham, with his parents, Albert a Police Superintendent and Mary his wife, together with one brother and one sister. He was employed as an auctioneer's clerk. His parents later moved to "La Roseraie" 59 Summerheath Road, Hailsham. Before joining up, Albert worked in Mr Barrett Terry's (Surveyor's) office at Eastbourne.

Albert enlisted into the Royal Sussex Regiment on the outbreak of war. He served as a Private with the 7th battalion, 12th Division. He subsequently gained a commission and became a second Lieutenant. He was wounded on 10 March 1917 and was in hospital in France for two months. It was then that he was made a full Lieutenant, backdated to September 1916. He was originally reported as 'missing' but it was later confirmed that he had been killed in action near Twin Copse, Arras in the Pas de Calais Department of France on 4th July 1917, aged 25 years. His death is commemorated on the Arras memorial (*Memorial Ref: Bay 6*).

The French handed over Arras to Commonwealth forces in the spring of 1916 and the system of tunnels upon which the town is built were used and developed in preparation for the major offensive planned for April 1917. The Commonwealth section was begun in March 1916 and continued to be used by field ambulances and fighting units until November 1918. The cemetery was enlarged after the Armistice and now contains nearly 2,700 Commonwealth burials of WWI.

Having been brought up and educated in Hailsham, the name and rank of "*Lieutenant A.E. Willard*" appears on the Hailsham Boys School Memorial board. His name also appears on the Memorial board in St Mary's Church, Hailsham as well as in the 'Roll of Honour' printed earlier in the parish magazine.

൰൰൰൰൰൰൰൰൰൰

𝒲𝑜𝑜𝑑, 𝐹𝑟𝑎𝑛𝑘

Rank	Regiment	Age at Death
Private Corporal	(1) Royal Sussex (2) Royal Warwickshire	41yrs

Frank Wood was born at Hailsham in 1877, the son of William and Lucy Wood. In 1891, Frank, then aged 14 years, is living with his parents, William, a farm labourer and Lucy his wife at 5 Garfield Place, Hailsham. He was employed as a baker's boy. In 1911, Frank, then aged 34 years and still single, was living with his parents, this time at 30 Garfield Road, Hailsham. He was employed as a general labourer. He subsequently got a job in the twine department of Burfield & Son, Rope and Twine factory in South Road, Hailsham.

Frank was in the Territorials at the start of the war and was still employed at Burfield's when he enlisted at the Hailsham Recruiting Office into the Royal Sussex Regiment. He served as a Private (*Service No: 1394*) in France and Flanders. He subsequently transferred into the Royal Warwickshire Regiment where he rose to become a Corporal (*Service No: TF/242039*) with the 2/6th Battalion, 61st Division. He was killed in action on 24th October 1918 and is buried in Crucifix Cemetery, Vendegies-sur-Ecaillon in France (*Grave Ref: A.15*).

Vendegies-sur-Ecaillon is a village and commune in the Department of the Nord, in the valley of the Ecaillon, 12 kilometres south of Valenciennes and 10 kilometres west of Le Quesnoy. The village was captured by the 19th (Western) and 61st (South Midland) Divisions on 24 October 1918, after severe fighting. The cemetery stands behind a roadside crucifix, which was made by the 61st Division after the battle. The cemetery contains 50 Commonwealth burials of WWI, 31 of them belonging to the 2nd/6th Royal Warwickshires.

Having been brought up and educated in Hailsham, the name and rank of "*Corporal F. Wood*" appears on the Hailsham Boys School Memorial board. His name also appears on the Memorial board in St Mary's Church, Hailsham as well as in the 'Roll of Honour' printed earlier in the parish magazine. Being an employee of Burfield's, his name appears in the 'Roll of Honour' in their Factory Record and Visitors book, under the heading "*The Factory Recorder*".

஦஦஦஦஦஦஦஦஦஦

Wood, John

Rank	Regiment	Age at Death
Petty Officer	HMS "Flirt"	26yrs

John Wood was born at Herstmonceux in 1890, the son of John and Harriett Wood. In 1901, John Wood, aged 11 years, was living with his family at Newcastle, Dallington. In 1911, he is aged 21 years, single and described as a farmer's son working on a farm, living with his parents, John & Harriett, one brother and one sister at Grovelye Farm, Dallington.

It is believed that this is the right John Wood. There are no other people of this name living in the Hailsham area on either the 1901 or 1911 census records. The name and rank of *"Petty Officer J. Wood"* appears on the Hailsham Council Boys School Memorial board and therefore he must have been at least educated in Hailsham.

His name also appears on the Memorial board at St Mary's Church, Hailsham and in the 'Roll of Honour', printed earlier in parish magazine, which shows *"John Wood - 1st class Petty Officer on HMS Flirt"*. Commonwealth War Graves Commission records reveal that he was Chief Stoker (*Service No: 170070*) and that he served on HMS "Flirt".

HMS "Flirt" had a complement of 63 men and was sunk in the Battle of Dover Strait on the night of 27 October 1916. The German Navy had mounted a raid in the Dover Straits against the ships of the awesome Dover Patrol who were maintaining the Dover Barrage (*This was a minefield*). Twelve German Destroyers in two divisions of six broke into the barrage and sunk seven of the attendant trawlers and drifters.

HMS "Flirt" investigated this incident and, although she sighted the enemy, the ship mistook them for Allied Destroyers returning to Dover. HMS Flirt stopped to rescue survivors of the drifters in the sea and put her searchlight on to do this. Meanwhile the Germans returned and a well-aimed torpedo struck the ship amidships. She sunk immediately with a loss of most of the crew, the only survivors being those in the lifeboat, which was engaged in picking up other survivors. John Wood was not amongst those who survived this tragedy and he was drowned on 27 October 1916. His name is commemorated on the Portsmouth Naval Memorial (*Memorial Ref: 15*).

இஇஇஇஇஇஇஇஇஇ

Part Two – The Great War: 1914-18

Woodhams, Albert J.

Rank	Regiment	Age at Death
Private	Suffolk	23yrs

Albert John Woodhams was born in Hellingly in 1896, the son of Albert and Anne Woodhams. In 1901, whilst his parents and three sisters are shown as living at Marshfoot Cottages in Hailsham, Albert himself is not mentioned. Ten years later, however, Albert, then aged 15 years, is shown living with his parents Albert, a farmer's son (*sic*) and Anne his wife, together with his one brother and two sisters at Rosemount, Harebeating in Hailsham. He was employed as a milkman on a farm. His parents later moved to Havelock House, Battle Road, Hailsham.

Albert enlisted at the Eastbourne Recruiting Office in August 1916 into the Suffolk Regiment. He served as a Private (*Service No: 50449*) with the 2nd Battalion, 3rd Division. He went to France just before Christmas 1916. He was wounded twice in action and sent home to England on both occasions. On the third occasion, he was badly wounded in the head, admitted unconscious to hospital in the early hours of the day but died of his wounds five hours later on 27th September 1918, aged 23 years. He is buried in Sunken Road Cemetery, Boisleux-St Marc in the Pas de Calais Department of France (*Grave Ref: II.F.30*). This area was occupied by Commonwealth troops in March 1917 following the German withdrawal to the Hindenburg Line. Several Casualty Clearing Stations were established around there but they had gone by the end of March 1918 as the area was back in German hands. In September, the situation had changed back again. Sunken Road Cemetery was begun in May 1917 and used until July when it began to be shelled. It was completed the following October and now contains over 400 Commonwealth burials

Having been brought up and educated in Hailsham, the name and rank of "*Private A.J. Woodhams*" appears on the Hailsham Boys School Memorial board. His name also appears on the Memorial board in St Mary's Church, Hailsham as well as in the 'Roll of Honour' printed earlier in the parish magazine. His death is commemorated by a memorial inscription on his

parent's grave in Hailsham Cemetery (*Space No 3884*). Being a member of the Weslyan congregation, he is commemorated on the Memorial tablet in Hailsham Methodist Church where he was locally known as Charles.

ഇ ഇ ഇ ഇ ഇ ഇ ഇ ഇ ഇ ഇ

Part Two – The Great War: 1914-18

The Battle of Aubers Ridge

The battle of Aubers Ridge took place on 9th May 1915 in French Flanders, which word means 'flooded ground'. It was the British contribution to the Allied spring offensive of 1915 and was fought over the same ground as the battle of Neuve Chapelle, some two months earlier. This had only been successful due to a preliminary 40 minute shell bombardment. The battle of Aubers Ridge turned out to be a disastrous failure due to a gross shortage of artillery ammunition (referred to subsequently as the "*shell scanda*l") and a complete under-estimation of the strength of the German positions.

Since the battle of Neuve Chapelle, the Germans had greatly strengthened their lines. Their soldiers had worked with feverish intensity and the additional troops meant that they were not only extremely well prepared but also stronger on the ground than they had been before. Aubers Ridge itself, is barely discernible but it gave a significant observation point for the enemy looking west over the British front.

The British attack was launched by General Haig, aimed at the Ridge. It was intended to send in two attacks with the hope that they could meet up behind the German front lines. General Haig had requested extra artillery to increase the strength of the bombardment planned for that day but all available artillery reserves had been sucked into the fighting at the second battle of Ypres, still raging to the north. In addition, ammunition shortage had been a problem since the opening stages of the war and was, by now, particularly acute.

The preliminary bombardment started at 5am, the field artillery pounding the barbed wire with shrapnel shells, whilst the howitzers showered the trenches with large calibre shells. At 5.30am, on 9th May 1915, after only 30 minutes of preliminary bombardment, the British troops went 'over the top'. The German sentries quickly spotted the men leaving the trenches and began cutting them to shreds with machine gun fire. Despite this, the British rushed forward as they were ordered to do and those that survived managed to gain a line not far ahead. Unfortunately, the survivors were pinned down in no-mans land and were either cut down or impaled on the barbed wire defences. At 6am, the order was given to stop the attack but the German artillery then started shelling both no-mans land and the British front line. By the morning of 10 May 1915, all hopes of renewing the attack were abandoned because of a lack of shells and, above all, the huge numbers of casualties.

In one single day, the British Army had lost 11,000 men, the vast majority within yards of their own front-line trench. Hailsham lost the lives of 4 brave men on that dreadful day: - Charles Hollebon, Edgar Rigglesford, George Smith and John Tingley. (*However, it was worse for the village of Wadhurst who reportedly lost 24 men that day.*)

ꑭꑭꑭꑭꑭꑭꑭꑭꑭꑭ

Part Three – World War II

"Details of the Fallen – WW II"

The following section provides a brief glimpse into the personal lives and military careers of the 35 men whose names are commemorated on Hailsham's war memorial. This draws upon more recent times, of course, and many of the relatives are still living, some still in Hailsham. Whilst the majority were either born or brought up in the town or were living in or near the town before the war, other factors have sometimes come into play to connect these men with Hailsham.

In compiling these records, information has been gained from sources such as local newspapers, particularly the Sussex Express, street directories as well as personal knowledge and photographs kindly given and shared by descendants of their families. Once again, it is unfortunate that the records, which were made at the time, particularly those that would show the reasons for including their names on the memorial, who these people were and what connection they had with Hailsham, are no longer in existence. St Mary's Church Parish magazines covering the war years should also have been a valuable source of information but they also appear to be no longer in existence.

Bayley, Edward A.

Rank	Regiment	Age at Death
Sergeant (Pilot)	R.A.F. - 249 Squadron	29yrs

Edward Alan Bayley was born in March 1911 at Eastbourne, the son of Edward George and Edith Bayley. He apparently had an early interest in flying as he gained his flying certificate with the Sussex Aero Club on an Avro Avian Hermes 11 in November 1933. The Club records also show that he was a fur farmer and was living at Lindisfarne, Heathfield. Edward got married and was latterly living with his wife, Josephine Adele Bayley, at 'Hemsley', 15 London Road, Hailsham.

Edward was conscripted and joined the RAF Volunteer Reserve where he served with 249 Squadron (*Service No: 741004*). This squadron had been reformed in May 1940 as a fighter squadron at Church Fenton, initially with Spitfires but after a few weeks it was re-equipped with Hurricanes. The squadron became operational in July 1940 and flew defensive patrols before moving south in August to take part in the Battle of Britain. Edward rose to become a sergeant (pilot).

Edward died on 10 October 1940 aged 29 years. This might have been the result of a flying accident or he could have been killed whilst in the plane, which was returning from a sortie. He was buried in Bromley (St Luke's) Cemetery, Kent (*Grave Ref: Section K Grave 198*).

෮෮෮෮෮෮෮෮෮෮

Part Three – World War II

Beardmore, Clement M.

Rank	Regiment	Age at Death
Private Lance Corporal	(1) Royal Sussex (2) Parachute	22yrs

Clement Maxton Beardmore was born in 1922, the second son of Edward Arthur and Minnie Beardmore who lived at "Lyndale", 40 South Road in Hailsham. Prior to joining the army, Clement served in the National Fire Service.

He was conscripted at the start of the war and drafted into the Royal Sussex Regiment. He served in the Middle East Force until after the El Alamein engagement, when he volunteered for parachute duty. After training, he joined the Parachute Regiment, Army Air Corps (*Service No: 6410619*). He served in the 10th Battalion, which was a war-formed unit formed from the 2nd Battalion, Royal Sussex Regiment and also one of the first units to enter Italy. Clement rose to become a Lance Corporal. He was wounded by a sniper during the Italian campaign and returned to England with the Battalion. He then trained with the signal section until they left for Arnhem.

The 10th battalion fought at the Battle of Arnhem in '*Operation Market Garden*', which was the largest airborne operation of all time. The 1st British Airborne Division, which included the 1st, 2nd, 3rd, 10th, 11th and 156th battalions of the Parachute Regiment under the command of Major General R E Urquhart was dropped near Arnhem to seize the road bridge over the Neder Rijn. Approximately 3,500 survivors of the 1st Airborne Division established themselves in buildings and woods around Oosterbeek with the intention of holding a bridgehead on the north side of the Rhine. Throughout the day they were heavily attacked. Later information passed to his father showed that Clement had been at Arnhem for about four days after making a successful parachute drop. One morning, it was found necessary to move the jeep in which were the signal stores and the equipment which were the only means of communicating with Divisional Headquarters, as the enemy had closed in on it during the night. Lance Corporals Beardmore and Dunkerley volunteered to go out and get the jeep. As they reached it, the enemy laid on a barrage and since then, the two young parachutists had been reported missing.

It was eventually confirmed that Clement lost his life on 21 September 1944 at age 22 years. He was buried at Arnhem Oosterbeek war cemetery in the Netherlands (*Grave Ref: 5. A. 14*).

ꕔ ꕔ ꕔ ꕔ ꕔ ꕔ ꕔ ꕔ ꕔ ꕔ

Part Three – World War II

Boniface, Jack

Rank	Regiment	Age at Death
Able Seaman	H.M.S. "Hood"	18yrs

Jack Boniface was born in January 1923, the only son of Charlie and Ivy Emma Boniface who lived at no.15 Council Houses (later no.107) Mill Road in Hailsham. Jack was educated at Hailsham Council School and left at age 13½ years to join the training ship, "Arethusa". He was afterwards at the "St Vincent" training establishment.

Jack joined the Royal Navy when he was just 16 years old *Service No: P/JX 158220*). He served on the ill-fated HMS "Hood", an Admiral-class battle cruiser. He rose to the rank of Able Seaman.

In May 1941, the German battleship "Bismarck" with an escort sailed for the Atlantic and HMS "Hood", together with the battleship "Prince of Wales", was sent out in pursuit to intercept the German ships before they could break into the Atlantic and attack Allied convoys. The German ships were spotted by the British heavy cruisers on the 23rd May and HMS "Hood" caught up with the "Bismarck" and the heavy cruiser "Prinz Eugen", in the Denmark Strait between Greenland and Iceland on 24 May 1941. The action is referred to as the Battle of Denmark Strait. HMS "Hood" was sunk with the loss of 1,415 men and only 3 survivors. Jack Boniface, aged 18 years old, along with his Hailsham comrades Frank Erridge, Kenneth Funnell and Alfred Perrin died that day. (*Note - A more detailed account of this action can be found on pages 148 to 149.*) The irony of this was that Jack was on his last voyage with HMS "Hood" and was due to be posted/transferred to another ship when it docked.

Jack Boniface is also commemorated on the Portsmouth Naval Memorial (*Panel 47, Col 2*) and in the Hood Chapel, Church of St John the Baptist, Boldre, Hampshire.

༜༜༜༜༜༜༜༜༜༜

Part Three – World War II

Brook, Charles T.

Rank	Regiment	Age at Death
Able Seaman	H.M.S. "Edgehill" (X39)	40yrs

Charles Thomas Brook was born at Westham, in 1900, the son of Thomas and Ellen Gift Brook. In 1911, the family were living at 1 Victoria Terrace, Hankham. Charles was aged 11 years and still at school whilst his father was working as a platelayer for the Railway company.

Charles was conscripted and joined the Royal Navy (*Service No. C/J 38858*). He served on HMS "Edgehill" (X 39) and rose to the rank of Able Seaman. This ship was originally a merchant vessel, "Willamette Valley", but was requisitioned by the Royal Navy, converted to a decoy ship and commissioned as a special service vessel. The ship had a concealed armament of nine 4in guns, four torpedo tubes and carried a buoyant cargo to help keep her afloat if hit.

At 00.12hrs on 29 June 1940, the ship was struck amidships by one torpedo fired from a German submarine, U-51. The ship stopped but did not sink due to her buoyant cargo. The U-boat surfaced and fired a 'coup de grace' at 01.06 hours but it needed a third torpedo fired at 01.24 hours before the the vessel began to sink slowly by the stern. Although there were 24 survivors, Charles Brook was amongst the 15 crewmen who died on that day, 29 June 1940. He was aged 40 years.

Charles' name is also commemorated on the Chatham Naval Memorial (*Memorial Ref: 35, 1*).

ῼ ῼ ῼ ῼ ῼ ῼ ῼ ῼ ῼ ῼ

Brown, Edward E.

Rank	Regiment	Age at Death
Warrant Officer II	Royal Tank	27yrs

Edward Evan Brown was born in 1916. He married Doris Irene Elvy in December 1943 at St Mary's Parish Church, Hailsham. Edward was living in Hailsham prior to his marriage but he and his wife subsequently moved to Eastbourne.

Edward joined the army prior to the war, in around 1937 and was in the Middle East for six years. By October 1942, he had risen to a sergeant and his address was given as "Brooklyn", Station Road in Hailsham. He served with the Eighth Army in the North African campaign with the 1st Royal Tank Regiment, part of the Royal Armoured Corps (*Service No: 7887910*). He subsequently gained the rank of Warrant Officer Class II, Squadron Sergeant Major. He was mentioned in despatches for devotion to duty.

Edward was killed in action on 25 July 1944, shortly before his 28th birthday, on the same day as his brother-in-law, Sergeant Alfred Elvy, serving in the same Regiment was wounded. Edward was buried in Ranville War Cemetery, Calvados in France (*Grave No: IX.B.8.*)

ꙄꙄꙄꙄꙄꙄꙄꙄꙄꙄ

Erridge, Frank A.

Rank	Regiment	Age at Death
Telegraphist	H.M.S. "Hood"	20yrs

Frank Alfred Erridge was born in 1921, the elder son of Robert and Elizabeth Erridge who lived at 3 Railway Cottages, Station Road in Hailsham. Frank was educated at both Hailsham Council and Bexhill County schools and played cricket and football for the school teams. He joined the navy immediately on leaving school at 15½ years of age. After training, he joined the Royal Navy (*Service No: P/JX 151516*) and in early 1939 joined the ill-fated HMS "Hood", an Admiral-class battle cruiser. He took part in operations at Narvik and served as a telegraphist.

In May 1941, the German battleship "Bismarck" with an escort sailed for the Atlantic and HMS Hood, together with the battleship "Prince of Wales", was sent out in pursuit to intercept the German ships before they could break into the Atlantic and attack Allied convoys. The German ships were spotted by the British heavy cruisers on the 23rd May and HMS "Hood" caught up with the "Bismarck" and the heavy cruiser "Prinz Eugen", in the Denmark Strait between Greenland and Iceland on 24 May 1941. The action is referred to as the Battle of Denmark Strait. HMS "Hood" was sunk with the loss of 1,415 men and only 3 survivors. Frank Erridge, aged 20 years old, along with his Hailsham comrades Jack Boniface, Kenneth Funnell and Alfred Perrin died that day. (*Note - A fuller account of this action can be found on pages 148 to 149.*)

Frank Erridge is also commemorated on the Portsmouth Naval Memorial (*Panel 52, Col 3*) and in the Hood Chapel, Church of St John the Baptist, Boldre, Hampshire.

෴෴෴෴෴෴෴෴෴෴

Part Three – World War II

Fears, Leonard F.

Rank	Regiment	Age at Death
Private	Royal Sussex	26yrs

Leonard Frank Fears was born in 1918, the son of Emma Grace Fears, who lived at 9 Gordon Place in Hailsham. At one time, he was employed by his uncle, Mr Jesse Page at Brook Street Bakery in Polegate. He was a keen member of the Hailsham Young People's Fellowship. Leonard subsequently married Iris Alice Turner who lived at Ersham Cottage, Nursery Path, Hailsham. They set up home at 'Jaleen', Battle Road in Hailsham. Prior to joining the army, he was on the staff of the Co-Operative Stores at Hailsham.

Leonard was conscripted in February 1940 and joined the Royal Sussex Regiment (*Service No: 6403429*) where he served in the 1st Battalion. He went overseas in December 1943 and saw Active service in Italy as part of the Central Mediterranean theatre of war.

Following the fall of Rome to the Allies in June 1944, the German retreat was ordered and successive stands were made on a series of defensive lines. The last of these, the Gothic Line, was breached by the Allies during the Autumn campaign. The Front inched forward as far as Ravenna but divisions were transferred to support the new offensive in France. The Germans dug in to a number of key defensive positions and the advance stalled as winter set in. Coriano Ridge was the last important ridge in the way of the Allied advance in the Adriatic sector in the autumn of 1944. Its capture was the key to Rimini and eventually to the River Po. German parachute and panzer troops, aided by bad weather, resisted all attacks on their positions between 4 and 12 September 1944. On the night of 12 September the Eighth Army reopened its attack on the Ridge, with British and Canadian Armoured Divisions. This attack was successful in taking the Ridge, but marked the beginning of a week of the heaviest fighting experienced in this offensive.

Leonard was killed during this action on 26 September 1944, aged 26 years. He was buried at Coriano Ridge War Cemetery in Italy (*Grave No XVII. B.6*). Rev Chapman, the vicar of St Mary's Church, Hailsham, spoke warmly of both Leonard and his colleague, William Piper, in his Sunday sermon after their deaths had been officially confirmed.

שׁשׁשׁשׁשׁשׁשׁשׁשׁשׁ

Part Three – World War II

Fitzgerald, Michael P.

Rank	Regiment	Age at Death
Sub-Lieutenant	H.M.S. "Esk"	20yrs

Michael Papillon Fitzgerald was born in 1920, the son of Major N. D'Arcy Fitzgerald, R.A., and Mrs Kathleen Mary Fitzgerald who latterly lived at Park Cottage, The Avenue in Hailsham.

Michael joined the Royal Navy where he rose to the rank of Sub-Lieutanant. He served on HMS "Esk", which was an E-Class destroyer launched in 1934 by Swan Hunter and fitted as a minelayer. This ship was sunk by a mine during the Texel Disaster on the night of 31 August 1940.

This disaster took place off the Dutch coast and involved the sinking of two Royal Navy destroyers and damage to a third and light cruiser. The disaster was caused by a destroyer flotilla running into a newly laid and uncharted minefield, which caused serious damage to the vessel; two more destroyers were sunk going to the aid of the first and a light cruiser sent as an escort was slightly damaged by a mine on the return journey. HMS "Esk" was one of the two destroyers that went to the aid of the first destroyer and all aboard except for one man were killed. In all, the disaster caused around 300 deaths with a further 100 men either injured or taken prisoner of war.

Michael Fitzgerald, aged 20 years old, was one of the unfortunate men who lost their lives that fateful night of 31 August 1940. His death is also commemorated on the Portsmouth Naval Memorial (*Panel 37 Col 1*).

಄಄಄಄಄಄಄಄಄಄

Part Three – World War II

Fuller, Mark

Rank	Regiment	Age at Death
Private	Royal Sussex	33yrs

Frederick Mark Fuller (always known as 'Mark') was born on 21st September 1907 at East Dean, the son of Walter Fuller and his wife, Ruth, nee Boniface. Mark had three brothers. At some time, the family moved from East Dean to Downash Cottages in Hailsham and it was from there that Mark married Nellie Beatrice Saunders on 2 October 1926. The new couple moved to 99 Station Road in Hailsham and subsequently were to have six children. Mark was a prominent football player for Hailsham and possibly also played for Sussex.

Prior to the war, he worked as a farmer at Rickney Farm near Hailsham. Being in farming should have meant that he was exempt from National Service. However, he had previously joined the Territorials and was therefore 'called up'. He joined the Royal Sussex Regiment and served as a Private (*Service No: 6397322*) with the 7th Battalion. He went over to France as part of the Expeditionary Force. Mark was killed on 20 May 1940 aged 33 years at Abbeville, in France.

For much of the First World War, Abbeville was headquarters of the Commonwealth lines of communication and No. 3 BRCS, No.5 and No.2 Stationary Hospitals were stationed there variously from October 1914 to January 1920. The Communal Cemetery was used for burials from November 1914 to September 1916, the earliest being made among the French military graves. During the early part of the Second World War, Abbeville was a major operational aerodrome but the town fell to the Germans at the end of May 1940. It was during this action that Mark lost his life.

He was buried at Abbeville Communal Cemetery Extension, in France (*Grave No: Plot 9, Row D. Grave 11*).

ऴऴऴऴऴऴऴऴऴऴ

Part Three – World War II

Funnell, Kenneth

Rank	Regiment	Age at Death
Ordinary Seaman	H.M.S. "Hood"	18yrs

Kenneth George Funnell was born on 5 September 1922, the eldest son of Kenneth and Edith Mabel Funnell who lived at 6 Cobden Place in Hailsham. He was educated at Hailsham Council Boys School where he used to play cricket. He left when he was 14½ years old initially to join the naval training ship "Arethusa". He subsequently went to "HMS Ganges" (*see photo*), both of which were the Navy's shore training establishments. During the first year these boys were quickly made into men with a sound foundation and knowledge of their future profession and, following a further six months specialist training, they were ready to go to sea and be part of a ship's company. Kenneth enlisted into the Royal Navy at 16½ years (*Service No: P/JX 158107*) and served on the ill-fated HMS "Hood", an Admiral-class battle cruiser. He was an Ordinary Seaman.

In May 1941, the German battleship "Bismarck" with an escort sailed for the Atlantic and HMS "Hood", together with the battleship Prince of Wales, was sent out in pursuit to intercept the German ships before they could break into the Atlantic and attack Allied convoys. The German ships were spotted by the British heavy cruisers on the 23rd May and HMS "Hood" caught up with the "Bismarck" and the heavy cruiser "Prinz Eugen", in the Denmark Strait between Greenland and Iceland on 24 May 1941. The action is referred to as the Battle of Denmark Strait. HMS "Hood" was sunk with the loss of 1,415 men and only 3 survivors. Kenneth Funnell, aged 18 years, along with his Hailsham comrades Jack Boniface, Frank Erridge and Alfred Perrin died that day. (*Note - A fuller account of this action can be found on pages 148 to 149.*)

His death is also commemorated on the Portsmouth Naval Memorial (*Panel 50 Col 2*) and in the Hood Chapel, Church of St John the Baptist, Boldre, Hampshire.

卍 卍 卍 卍 卍 卍 卍 卍 卍 卍

Part Three – World War II

Haffenden, Maurice E.

Rank	Regiment	Age at Death
Sergeant	R.A.F. - 77 Squadron	25yrs

Maurice Ernest Haffenden was born at Marle Green, Heathfield on 1st April 1918 the son of Clifford and Mabel Haffenden. The family subsequently moved to Hailsham, lived at various local addresses but latterly at "Ivanhoe", Hawthylands Road. Maurice went to School at Hailsham Council Boys School and, when he left, he entered local government and worked in the Town Clerk's Department of Hailsham Rural District Council.

At the start of the war, when he was living with his family at "Ivanhoe", Hawthylands Road in Hailsham, Maurice joined the Royal Air Force Volunteer Reserve. In August 1940 he was serving (*Service No: 911279*) with 43 Squadron, operating from Tangmere. This was a fighter base being used at that time for patrols over the Dunkirk beaches. In June 1942, Maurice was in Calgary, Canada being re-trained for bombers and, in particular, night-flying. On completion of this training, he returned to England and joined 77 Squadron, which formed part of Coastal Command. He rose to the rank of Sergeant. During August and September 1943, 77 Squadron attacked various German cities including Berlin and Nuremberg and suffered a great many casualties and lost aircraft. Maurice, a Navigator, was on one of these

bombing raids, when his plane was shot down over the North Sea as it was returning from Germany. The date was 23rd September 1943 and Maurice was 25 years old. He was unmarried with just one sister, Mizpah (*'Babs'*).

His war service earned him the Air Crew of Europe Star, which was awarded to him as a crew member who flew operationally over Europe from a UK air base. He was also awarded the 1939/45 Star and the British Defence Medal. His body was never recovered.

Maurice's death is also commemorated on the Runnymede Memorial (*Panel 151*).

卐 卐 卐 卐 卐 卐 卐 卐 卐 卐

Part Three – World War II

Helsdon, Raymond A.

Rank	Regiment	Age at Death
Captain	General List	35yrs

Raymond Athol Helsdon was born in London in March 1909, the son of Horace John and Flora Jane Helsdon. After Raymond left school, he worked in Canada for a year before returning to England and joining the East Sussex Constabulary. He married Lydia Rapson, (*his former landlady's daughter*) at Lewes on 1 September 1932. In the days when most places had their own local policeman, Raymond and Lydia lived in various towns and villages throughout East Sussex. They had three sons, Robin, born 1934 who died in infancy, Derek, born 1935, and David born 1942. Raymond rapidly gained promotion and eventually become the youngest Divisional Inspector in the history of the East Sussex Constabulary. He was posted to Hailsham where the family lived in the former Police Station next to the Methodist Church.

In 1943, Inspector Helsdon, thinking he was not doing enough on the Home Front, enlisted in the General List with the rank of Captain (*Service No: 313592*) as part of the British Expeditionary Force. His unit, European Civil Affairs was created to follow the Allied Invasion forces and re-establish the municipal administration of towns and villages as they were liberated from the Nazis. An interesting account of his work is contained in a letter sent by him on 29 September 1944, an extract from which is given on page 168. Raymond was tragically killed in a motor accident on 15 October 1944 when he was walking along a country lane near Eupen, in Belgium. He was aged 35 years and, at the time of his death, was working in the German border town of Aachen.

He is buried at Hotton War Cemetery in Belgium, which contains 666 Commonwealth burials of the Second World War (*Grave Ref: II.C.2*). The village of Hotton was the western limit of the great German counter offensive in the Ardennes. He is commemorated in a plaque on the wall of the Hailsham Methodist Church in the High Street, Hailsham with which the family maintained close links. Lydia Helsdon and her sons subsequently lived in Battle Road, Summerfields Avenue and Bellbanks Road in Hailsham.

〇〇〇〇〇〇〇〇〇〇

Hide, Henry

Rank	Regiment	Age at Death
Lieutenant	Royal Artillery	32yrs

Henry Hide was the younger (surviving) son of Charles and Mildred Hide who came from Eastbourne but latterly lived at "Veryan", Summerfields Avenue, Hailsham. Henry was educated at Roborough School in Eastbourne and became an optician working at Fareham in Hampshire. He joined the Territorials in 1938.

Henry was called up on the outbreak of war and enlisted into the Royal Artillery (*Service No: 155348*) where he served in the 95th Light Anti-Aircraft Regiment. He received his commission in November 1940 and gained the rank of Lieutenant. He was in France for a short time in 1944 before being placed with an anti-aircraft battery.

It appears that he was seriously wounded in action and brought back to England for treatment and to convalesce. He was at Addenbrookes Hospital in Cambridge when he tragically died on 15 February 1945. His body was brought back to Hailsham and he was buried in Hailsham Cemetery (*Grave space: 2537*)

וกุוกุוกุוกุוกุוกุוกุוกุוกุ

Part Three – World War II

Jarvis, Robin

Rank	Regiment	Age at Death
Private	Highland Light Infantry	19yrs

Robin Jarvis was born in 1926, the son of Robert and Dora Kathleen Jarvis who lived at "Virginia", Carters Corner Road, near Hailsham. As a boy, he attended Herstmonceux Day School and prior to joining the army, he was employed by Mr R.S. Harmer, baker of Windmill Hill.

In April 1944, Robin was conscripted into the Highland Light Infantry (City of Glasgow Regiment). He served as a Private (Service No: 14753002) in the 1st Battalion. In February 1945, he went overseas to serve with the British Liberation Army. The 1st Battalion of the Liberation Army went to France in 1939 as part of the British Expeditionary Force fighting during the withdrawal to Dunkirk and was eventually evacuated. After four years in Britain it returned to France as part of the 53rd (Welsh) Division, landing in Normandy towards the end of June 1944. Their last battle before the final advance into Germany was the battle of the Reichswald, which ended in March 1945 and it was probably in the aftermath of this battle that Robin lost his life.

Robin was killed in action on 5th April 1945, less than two weeks after his 19th birthday. Unfortunately, no further information is available on his life. He was buried in Reichswald Forest War Cemetery near Kleve in Germany (*Grave Ref: 61. B. 5*).

ഇ ഇ ഇ ഇ ഇ ഇ ഇ ഇ ഇ ഇ

Part Three – World War II

Kauter, Herman J.

Rank	Regiment	Age at Death
Captain	Royal Tank	31yrs

Herman Joseph Kauter was born in 1909, the son of Herman and Ida Kauter. Neither he, nor his parents are apparent in the 1911 census and so his nationality is uncertain. His parents appear to have emigrated to Australia at a later date.

He subsequently got married as records show that his wife's name was Elizabeth Audrey who came from Eastbourne. It is currently assumed that they either lived somewhere around Hailsham or that Herman or his wife worked in the area.

Joseph joined the Royal Tank Regiment, Royal Armoured Corps. He was commissioned and served as Captain, Adjutant (*Service No: 50227*) with the 7th Brigade in the France and Belgium Campaign. The Battle of Arras took place on 21 May 1940. It was an Allied counter-attack against the flank of the German forces which were pushing north towards the Channel coast to entrap the Allied forces who were advancing east into Belgium. Seventy four British tanks, under Major-General Franklyn met up with German army under *Generalmajor* Erwin Rommel. The British attack and further French support attacks were repulsed, resulting in a German victory. The British lost about 35 tanks out of the 74, with 50-75 killed or wounded and 170 were taken prisoner. The French lost about 20 of their tanks.

Herman Kauter was killed in this action on 21 May 1940, aged 31 years. He was buried at Longuenesse (St Omer) Souvenir Cemetery, near St Omer in France (*Grave Ref: Plot 8. Row B. Grave 6*).

ཉ ཉ ཉ ཉ ཉ ཉ ཉ ཉ ཉ ཉ

Part Three – World War II

King, George E.

Rank	Regiment	Age at Death
Private Private	(1) Royal Sussex (2) Dorsetshire	18yrs

George Ethelbert (Edward) King was born in Hailsham in June 1927, the younger of the two sons of George Henry and Annie Ethel King who also had four daughters. George did not like his middle name and so usually used the second name of Edward. The family originally lived in Garfield Road, Hailsham but, in the mid 1930s, moved to 95 Station Road, Hailsham. After leaving Hailsham Senior School, George was employed in the butchery department of the Hailsham Co-Operative Stores in the High Street until he joined the Army. Before he joined up, he was a sergeant in the Hailsham Army Cadet unit (*See photo*) before transferring to the local Home Guard.

He was conscripted in July 1944, just after his 18th birthday and he joined the Royal Sussex Regiment (*Service No: 14804695*). He went overseas on 13th February 1945 and was subsequently transferred to the Dorsetshire Regiment. He served as a Private in the 5th Battalion in the Western Europe Campaign of 1944/45.

George was killed in action on 29 April 1945 aged 18 years just a week before VE (*Victory in Europe*) Day. The Regiment crossed the Rhine by assault craft in the final drive of the war and this took them across northern Germany eventually to Bremerhaven on the North Sea coast. It was during this action when they were very close to their objective, that George was killed. He was buried at Becklingen War Cemetery in the north of Germany (*Grave Ref: 2.D.1A*). The site of this cemetery was chosen because it overlooked Luneberg Heath where, on 4 May 1945, VE Day, Field-Marshal Montgomery accepted the German surrender from Admiral Doenitz. This cemetery contains nearly 2,400 burials of the 2nd World War.

The additional tragedy is that, on VE Day, his family went to the Railway Tavern in Station Road, Hailsham to celebrate the end of the war and also the fact that both sons had survived (*or so they thought*) such terrible atrocities. The telegram notifying his parents that he had been killed was not received until a week after their celebration.

ꙍꙍꙍꙍꙍꙍꙍꙍꙍꙍ

Part Three – World War II

Langley, Walter

Rank	Regiment	Age at Death
Sergeant	Royal Marines	36yrs

Walter Langley was born in 1908, the third son of Alfred and Edith Mary Langley who latterly lived at 111 South Road, Hailsham. Walter left home, got married and lived with his wife at 18 Ersham Road in Hailsham. They had two daughters. Walter was employed as a postman attached to the Hailsham Post Office.

He enlisted into the Royal Marines several years prior to the outbreak of war and was called up on the Reserve in August 1939. He rose to the rank of Sergeant. One of the ships on which he was serving was 'blown up' off Crete. On this occasion, Walter was rescued after being 4½ hours in the water.

In 1944, he was serving on S.S. "Ascot", a 7,005 ton armed cargo steamer with 56 crew . On 29th February 1944, the ship was in the Indian Ocean en-route from Calcutta to Mauritius and about 800 miles North West of Diego Suarez. At 11.30am, the Japanese Submarine, I-37, fired two torpedoes at the ship. One hit the engine room killing four sailors and stopping the steamer dead in the water. The remaining crew abandoned ship and 52 survivors boarded a lifeboat and a raft. The submarine surfaced and, after a brief interrogation of the Captain and the Chief Officer, first scuttled the wreck of the "Ascot" with shell-fire and then machine-gunned the survivors in the lifeboat, thus sinking it. Only 4 sailors and 3 gunners were rescued some three days later by a Dutch steamer. Walter Langley was amongst those killed in action on 29 February 1944 aged 36 years.

His death is also commemorated on the Chatham Naval Memorial (*Memorial Ref: 79, 1*)as well as being commemorated on his parent's grave in Hailsham Cemetery (*Grave Space No: 2322*).

Note - After the war, the submarine commander concerned was convicted of several War Crimes, one of which was his action on this fateful day.

Part Three – World War II

Lovell, Wilfred A.

Rank	Regiment	Age at Death
Private	Queen's Royal (West Surrey)	35yrs

Wilfred Amos Lovell was born in June 1909, the eldest son of Amos and Winifred Lovell who lived at 82 High Street in Hailsham. He was a butcher by trade. At one time he worked for his father and prior to being called up, he was employed at Guildford and Uckfield. For a number of seasons, he played cricket for the Hailsham Club and was a very useful bowler. He was also a good billiards player and, on one occasion, won the Championship at the Memorial Institute.

William was called up around January 1942 and joined the Queen's Royal Regiment (West Surrey). He served as a Private (*Service No: 6105918*) with the 1/5th Battalion. He went overseas around April 1942.

He took part in the North African campaign and also saw service in Sicily and Italy. He was killed in action on 18th June 1944, aged 35 years.

The Allied offensive in north-western Europe began with the Normandy landings of 6 June 1944. There was heavy and fluctuating fighting in the vicinity of Tilly-sur-Seulles immediately after the landings involving chiefly the 49th and 50th Divisions. Tilly itself was not captured until 19 June 1944 and fighting continued nearby until mid July. It was during this action that Wilfred lost his life.

Wilfred Lovell is buried in Tilly-Sur-Seulles War Cemetery near Calvados in France (*Grave Ref: XI. F. 5*). This cemetery contains 990 Commonwealth burials of the Second World War and 232 German graves.

ꖛ ꖛ ꖛ ꖛ ꖛ ꖛ ꖛ ꖛ ꖛ ꖛ

129

Part Three – World War II

Mitchell, Kenneth T.W.

Rank	Regiment	Age at Death
Sergeant Air Gunner	R.A.F. – 36 Squadron	21yrs

Kenneth Thomas William Mitchell was born in 1920, probably at Upper Dicker where the family were living at the time. He was the eldest of the three sons of Mr & Mrs Tom Mitchell. The family moved to Hailsham in 1928 and they lived at 103 Mill Road in Hailsham. Tom went to school initially at Upper Dicker but subsequently attended Hailsham Council School. His father was a foreman for East Sussex County Council roadways and also a war Reserve special constable. Kenneth was an active member of the 1st Hailsham scout troop.

Kenneth obtained a scholarship to Bexhill County Grammar School and, whilst there, passed the entrance examination for the Royal Air Force. In 1936, he joined the Royal Air Force (*Service No: 570372*) as an Apprentice (*'Brats' as they were called*) and went to Cranwell, which was the RAF training school. On completion of his training, he served with 36 Squadron and subsequently rose to become a Sergeant. He was on leave in 1939 but was suddenly recalled, shortly before war was declared, as the Squadron had been posted to Singapore. He sailed to Singapore on the Troopship "*Dunera*", in a convoy escorted by HMS "*Ajax*", "*Dauntless*" and "*Exeter*".

In Singapore, he served as a wireless operator and air gunner on, what were then, "*ageing*" bi-planes, "Vickers Vildebeest", the only torpedo bombers available in 1939 to the RAF. Kenneth was tragically killed in in a flying accident when his plane crashed in a storm on 23rd June 1941. This was shortly before the Japanese invaded. After his death, his parents were sent a list of his belongings but the Japanese invaded before anything could be sent home. Some of the Squadron did manage to escape to Australia and sent his parents photographs of the funeral.

Kenneth is buried in Kranji War Cemetery, Singapore (*Grave No: 37.C.2*).

꒐꒐꒐꒐꒐꒐꒐꒐꒐꒐

Part Three – World War II

Moore, Frederick J.

Rank	Regiment	Age at Death
Leading Motor Mechanic	HM LST "413"	19yrs

Frederick John Moore was born in 1925, the eldest twin son of Frederick and Mercy Moore of Hailsham. Jack was in the choir at St Mary's Church whilst he was at Hailsham Council School. After leaving school, Jack was employed by Messrs Green Bros in the matting department. He joined the Hailsham and District Flight of the Air Training Corps on its formation in early 1941

Frederick was living with his parents at 9 Carrier's Path when he was called up in April 1942. He joined the Royal Navy (*Service No: C/MX550303*). He passed out as Leading Motor Mechanic in December 1943 and served on HM LST "413" . This ship was an LST class tank landing ship built in 1942 for the United States Navy. It was transferred to the United Kingdom and commissioned in January 1943 and ended its service in April 1946.

Frederick died on 13 May 1944 in a military hospital in the Isle of Wight where he had been admitted suffering from diphtheria. He was 19 years old. The funeral was conducted by Rev Chapman, the vicar at St Mary's Church and his coffin was covered by a Union Jack. A contingent of the A.T.C. Were present and they also formed a guard of honour at the Cemetery where the 'Last Post' was sounded.

Frederick was buried in Hailsham Cemetery (*Grave Space: 3428*) in one of the five WW II graves maintained by the Commonwealth War Graves Commission.

ꑛ ꑛ ꑛ ꑛ ꑛ ꑛ ꑛ ꑛ ꑛ ꑛ

Part Three – World War II

Newnham, Thomas H.

Rank	Regiment	Age at Death
Private Lance Sergeant	(1) Royal Sussex (2) Beds & Herts	36yrs

Thomas Harold Newnham was born at Horsted Keynes, on 11 March 1908, the son of Henry and Annie Newnham. Thomas grew up around Haywards Heath. At the age of 17 years, he joined the Royal Sussex Regiment and served in the regiment for eight years, several of which were spent in India. On 20 April 1933, he married Nancy Hilda Cousens at Hailsham. They set up home at 6 Francis Villas, Union Road in Hailsham. They had four children, three girls, one of whom died young and one boy. Prior to being called up, he was employed by the Weald Electricity Supply Company. He was a playing member of the Hailsham Football Club.

He was still on the reserve list at the outbreak of WW II and was transferred into the Bedfordshire and Hertfordshire Regiment. He served in the 2nd Battalion (*Service No: 6394826*). He went overseas in July 1943 and, by then, had risen to the rank of Lance Sergeant. He served in the Central Mediterranean theatre of war.

On 3 September 1943 the Allies invaded the Italian mainland, the invasion coinciding with an armistice made with the Italians who then re-entered the war on the Allied side. Progress through southern Italy was rapid despite stiff resistance, but the advance was checked for some months at the German winter defensive position known as the Gustav Line. This line eventually fell in May 1944 and as the Germans withdrew, the Allies took Rome on 3 June. From June and July 1944, the Germans were attempting to stop the Allied advance north of Rome in this region. Thomas was taking part in the advance. Tragically, he was shot by a sniper on 28 June 1944 aged 36 years. A fellow Sergeant wrote to his widow expressing sympathy and said that " *... it was largely due to his (Tom's) efforts that they were able to hold out in the face of enemy attacks at Cassino*".

Thomas Newnham was buried in Assisi War Cemetery in Italy (*Grave Ref: I. E. 11*). This cemetery contains 945 Commonwealth burials of the Second World War .

ꕊꕊꕊꕊꕊꕊꕊꕊꕊ

Perrin, Alfred J.

Rank	Regiment	Age at Death
Cook	H.M.S. "Hood"	29yrs

Alfred James Perrin was born on 29 December 1913, the only son of Mrs Ethel Perrin of "Corfu Cottages", Hawkswood in Hailsham. He was educated at Hailsham Council Boys School. When he left, he was employed by Mrs W.R. Angear of the Woolpack Hotel, Herstmonceux. For a number of seasons, he was a member of both the Hellingly Cricket and Football Clubs, acting as wicket-keeper and playing in goal.

Alfred was a baker by trade and enlisted into the Royal Navy (*Service No: P/MX 56031*) in March 1940. About six months later, he was drafted onto the ill-fated HMS "Hood", an Admiral-class battle cruiser where he was a cook.

In May 1941, the German battleship "Bismarck" with an escort sailed for the Atlantic and HMS "Hood", together with the battleship "Prince of Wales", was sent out in pursuit to intercept the German ships before they could break into the Atlantic and attack Allied convoys. The German ships were spotted by the British heavy cruisers on the 23rd May and HMS "Hood" caught up with the "Bismarck" and the heavy cruiser "Prinz Eugen", in the Denmark Strait between Greenland and Iceland on 24 May 1941. The action is referred to as the Battle of Denmark Strait. HMS "Hood" was sunk with the loss of 1,415 men and only 3 survivors. Alfred Perrrin, aged 29 years, along with his Hailsham comrades Jack Boniface, Frank Erridge and Kenneth Funnell died that day. (*Note - A detailed account of this action can be found on pages 148 to 149.*)

Alfred Perrin's death is also commemorated on the Portsmouth Naval Memorial (*Panel 57 Column 3*) and in the Hood Chapel, Church of St John the Baptist, Boldre, Hampshire. A photograph of him appears on the HMS "Hood" website.

ﬔﬔﬔﬔﬔﬔﬔﬔﬔﬔ

Part Three – World War II

Pettigrew, Herbert

Rank	Regiment	Age at Death
Sergeant	Royal Artillery	30yrs

Herbert Pettigrew was a British Subject born in India in 1914. At some time during the next few years, the family returned to England. Herbert married around the mid 1930s and the new couple went to live at "Santiago", 71 Mill Road in Hailsham. They had three children, all boys.

Herbert joined the Royal Artillery (*Service No: 875663*) where he served in the East African Artillery in the East African theatre of the war. He was attached to the 301 Field Regiment and rose to the rank of Sergeant. He had a lucky escape early on when he was serving on a ship as part of a convoy and the ship was torpedoed and sunk. On this occasion, Herbert was saved. Having recovered from this, he was put on another boat, this time the "*Khedive Ismail*". This was a 7513-ton vessel built in 1922, which had been requisitioned for use as a troop-ship and, in 1944, again formed part of a convoy.

Whilst off the Maldive Islands en route from Mombasa (Kenya) to Colombo (Sri Lanka), the ship was torpedoed in the Indian Ocean at 14.33 hours, by the Japanese submarine I-27 (Captain Toshiaki Fukumura). The vessel was carrying 1,511 people including 178 crew, 996 officers and men of the 301st Field Regiment, East African Artillery, 271 Royal Navy personnel and a detachment of 19 British Wrens. Also on board were 53 nursing sisters with one matron and 9 WTS ladies. It took less than two minutes for the ship to sink taking 1,297 of her passengers and crew with her. There were only 200 survivors. The submarine, I-27, was subsequently sunk by the escorting destroyers, HMS "Paladin" and "Petard". Herbert was not amongst the survivors and died on 12 February 1944, aged 30 years.

His death is also commemorated on the East Africa Memorial in Nairobi (*Column 2*).

೧೨೧೨೧೨೧೨೧೨೧೨೧೨೧೨೧೨

Part Three – World War II

Russell, Frank C.

Rank	Regiment	Age at Death
Gunner	Royal Artillery	32yrs

Frank Cecil Russell was born in North West London in 1910, the son of Elizabeth Russell.

He later got married. His wife's name was Jean who came from Eastbourne but originally came from Darlington in County Durham.

Frank joined the Royal Artillery. He served in the Middle East as a Gunner (*Service No: 1696533*) with 197 Battery as part of 61 Light Anti-Aircraft Regiment. It would appear that he took part in the Western Desert campaign in North Africa, which, in 1941, had reached a stalemate. The Allies took the opportunity to reorganise themselves and lthey aunched a new offensive, Operation Crusader, in November 1941. By January 1942, joint operations had resulted in the recapture of all of the territory only recently captured by the Germans and Italians. It was probably in the aftermath of this action that Frank lost his life.

He was killed on 20th January 1942, aged 32 years and is buried in Benghazi War Cemetery in Libya (*Grave Ref: 3. E. 13*). Benghazi was an important goal for both Allies and Axis forces during the Western Desert campaigns of 1942 and 1943. There are now 1,214 Commonwealth servicemen of the Second World War buried or commemorated in Benghazi War Cemetery.

卍 卍 卍 卍 卍 卍 卍 卍 卍 卍

Sargent, Charles W.

Rank	Regiment	Age at Death
Private	Duke of Cornwall's Light Infantry	18yrs

Charles William Sargent was born at Hailsham in 1926. He was the only son of Charles and Annie Sargent who lived at 134 South Road in Hailsham. 'Young Charlie', as he was called had two sisters, Marjorie who was older than him and Joyce who was younger. His mother died when he was quite young and his father later re-married and had two other daughters. 'Young Charlie' finished his education at Hailsham Senior School and then went to work for the Hailsham Co-Operative Stores. He subsequently worked for a short while for Mr W. Sims, a builder of Golden Cross, Chiddingly. In his spare time, he had joined the Hailsham Army Cadets but transferred to the local Home Guard a few weeks before he was 'called up'.

Charlie joined the Duke of Cornwall's Light Infantry in February 1944 when he was just 18 years old. He served (*Service No: 14712219*) as a Private in the 5th Battalion. In August 1944, he went overseas where he took part in the operation for the relief of the Airborne Troops at Arnhem. He then saw action in North-West Europe in the 1944/45 Campaign.

He was killed in action on 22nd November 1944 aged 18 years 10 months old. Initially, he was buried in a temporary grave (*see photo*) but his body was subsequently moved to the Reichswald Forest War Cemetery in Germany (*Grave Ref: 57. E. 7*). This cemetery was created after the Second World War when burials were brought in from all over western Germany and is the largest Commonwealth cemetery in the country.

Part Three – World War II

Saunders, Alan B.R.

Rank	Regiment	Age at Death
Gunner	Royal Artillery	26yrs

Alan Benjamin Robert Saunders was born in 1917, the son of Alan Robert and May Annette Saunders who lived at 21 Windsor Road in Hailsham. The family subsequently moved to 3 Mill Walk Cottages, No.82 Mill Road in Hailsham. Alan was educated at Hailsham Council School and, on leaving, he worked at the premises of Messrs Green Brothers. He joined the Hailsham Territorial Battery in 1938.

Alan was mobilised two days before hostilities opened and joined the Royal Artillery. He was attached (*Service No: 877147*) to the HQ, 50th Division. He served in France as part of the British Expeditionary Force and was evacuated through Dunkirk. Around July 1942, he went overseas again and took part in the campaign from Egypt to Tunisia. He saw active service in Sicily, serving with the Central Mediterranean Force.

Dvr. A. B. R. Saunders, R.A., of 3. Millwall Cottages. Mill-road, Hailsham.

On 10 July 1943, following the successful conclusion of the North Africa campaign, a combined allied force of 160,000 troops invaded Sicily as a prelude to the main assault on mainland Italy. Whilst the Italians offered little resistance and were shortly to re-enter the war on the side of the allies, the German opposition was strong and vigorous. Alan Saunders took part in this action. He was initially reported as missing but an official notification later confirmed that he had been killed on 14th July 1943, aged 26 years. He is buried in Syracuse War Cemetery, Sicily (*Grave Ref: VII. C. 7*). This photograph shows the original grave and its marker before it was replaced with a more permanent Memorial stone.

൰൰൰൰൰൰൰൰൰൰

Sea-Mays, Henry T.

Rank	Regiment	Age at Death
Second Officer	S.S. "Empire Moat"	65yrs

Henry Thomas Sea Mays (usually known just as Harry Mays) was born about 1876. As a child, he lived in Russia as his mother was on the household staff of the Czar.

Harry joined the Merchant Navy in about 1896 when he would have been 20 years old. He served in the Merchant Navy for the next 45 years, practically the whole of the time on the ships of Messrs Watts, Watts & Co Ltd.

He was married and had two sons, the eldest, Harry, who later joined the R.A.F and the youngest, Lewis, who later joined the Royal Navy. In 1941, he and his wife were living at "May Cottage", Mill Road, in Hailsham. Harry held the rank of Second Officer (*First Mate*) and, at the time, was serving on the SS "Empire Moat", which was an ore carrier, managed by Watts, Watts & Co of London. On 20th September 1941, the ship was torpedoed by the German submarine, "U-124", and later sank. Harry was drowned along with the rest of the crew. The ironic part of this was that this voyage was going to be his last trip as he intended giving up the sea afterwards.

In a letter to his widow, the shipping company stated: - "*He was very well known and admired throughout the fleet, especially for his tremendous help in training junior officers. He will be missed by all here a great deal and his place will be hard to fill.*"

Harry, aged 65 years lost his life on that day along with the rest of the crew. His death is also commemorated on the Tower Hill Memorial (*Panel 44*). His widow possibly remarried as she was later referred to as being Mrs E. Cornford of "May Cottage", Mill Road, Hailsham.

ΠΙ ΠΙ ΠΙ ΠΙ ΠΙ ΠΙ ΠΙ ΠΙ ΠΙ ΠΙ

Part Three – World War II

Skinner, Albert J.

Rank	Regiment	Age at Death
Leading Aircraftman	R.A.F.- Initial Training Wing	24yrs

Albert Jack Skinner (always known as Jack) was born at Barnet in London in 1917, the son of Albert and Mabel Skinner. He had a sister called Margaret. At an early stage in his life, the family moved to Hailsham, set up home at 87 South Road and Jack was educated at Hailsham Boys Council School. When he left school, Jack worked as a bricklayer with Thomas Rich, the builders of South Road, Hailsham.

On 24 April 1939, he changed his occupation and joined the Metropolitan Police. He was then over 21 years of age, which was the minimum age at that time for the Metropolitan Police. Having completed his training at Peel House, he served at Clapham 'nick'. He spent three years with the Force and, during this time he met Constance Waite who came from Southampton. They were married on 4 August 1941 at St James Church at Shirley in Southampton and it was almost at the same time that he volunteered for the Royal Air Force.

Service in the Metropolitan Police was a reserved occupation, which debarred serving officers from joining the armed forces. However, the rules were later relaxed and younger members of the Force were permitted to volunteer, which Jack did. He was one of the first to join the RAF (*Service No: 1389009*) under these rules. He took up training as a fighter pilot and joined No 11 Initial Training Wing based at Ansty, near Coventry.

He was tragically killed on 16 February 1942 aged 24 years old in a training accident, having only been in the Royal Air Force for six months. Jack's Commanding Officer wrote to his wife, expressing his condolences. He explained that the flying accident occurred when another aeroplane had collided with Jack's machine. He was rendered unconscious and taken straight to hospital but died later that day. He was buried at Southampton (Hollybrook) Cemetery (*Grave Ref: Section K. 10. Grave 205*).

רורורורורורורורורו

Stapley, William F.C.

Rank	Regiment	Age at Death
Sergeant	Royal Engineers	26yrs

William Frank George Stapley (usually referred to as 'Billie') was born in Sussex in August 1916, the eldest son of William Charles and Maud Stapley. When William was growing up, the family lived at "Lea Mount", Summerfields Avenue in Hailsham. Billie joined the 1st Hailsham Scout Troop and became a Rover Scout before eventually becoming Assistant Scoutmaster there. He also took part in productions of the Hailsham Conrose Players. He worked for Messrs Lovells, builders and decorators of Eastbourne. In October 1939, he married Gladys Kathleen Sands and they set up home at Monkhurst Cottages, Sandy Cross, Heathfield.

In December 1939, Billie joined the Royal Engineers (*Service No: 1902127*) where he saw service with the 1003 Docks Operating Company. This company was part of an operation to repair or install docks, which had been put out of action and were essential to the war effort. He was in France for six months and the Middle East for 2½ years. He rose through the ranks to become a Sergeant and was wounded in action whilst serving in Sicily. He subsequently died of his wounds in a casualty clearing station in Sicily.

On 10 July 1943, following the successful conclusion of the North Africa campaign, a combined allied force of 160,000 troops invaded Sicily as a prelude to the main assault on mainland Italy. Whilst the Italians offered little resistance and were shortly to re-enter the war on the side of the allies, the German opposition was strong and vigorous. It was 9 days later, on 19th July 1943, during this action that Billie lost his life, aged 26 years.

He was buried in the Syracuse War Cemetery in Sicily (*Grave Ref: I. F. 12*). His death is also commemorated by a memorial inscription on his parent's grave in Hailsham cemetery (*Grave space No: 4219*).

Part Three – World War II

Stonestreet, Frederick W.

Rank	Regiment	Age at Death
Gunner Corporal	(1) Royal Artillery (2) Cameronians (Scottish Rifles)	23yrs

Frederick William Stonestreet was born at Alfriston in 1922, the son of Vincent and Lucy Eleanor Stonestreet. The family moved to Hailsham in 1936 and lived at 1 Oaklands Cottages, Ersham Road, in Hailsham. He was a member of the Hailsham Territorial Battery of the Royal Artillery.

Frederick was mobilised at the outbreak of war and joined the Royal Artillery (*Service No: 874587*) where he served as a gunner with the 2nd battalion, the Cameronians (Scottish Rifles). He was with an anti-aircraft battery at Dover during the Battle of Britain. He left the country in May 1941 for Persia and was subsequently transferred to an infantry training depot in the Middle East. He was then drafted to the Cameronians and gained the rank of Corporal.

After service in Italy, he was transferred to the British Liberation Army as part of the Western Europe Campaign. He was killed in action on 21 April 1945 aged 23 years and was buried in Becklingen War Cemetery in the north of Germany (*Grave Ref: 18. C. 10*).

The site of this Cemetery was chosen for its position on a hillside, which overlooks Luneburg Heath, where Field-Marshal Montgomery accepted the German surrender on 4 May 1945. Burials were brought into the cemetery from isolated sites in the countryside, small German cemeteries and prisoner of war camps cemeteries, including the Fallingbostel cemetery, within a radius of about 80 kilometres. Most of those buried in the cemetery died during the last two months of the war. Becklingen War Cemetery contains 2,374 Commonwealth burials of the Second World War, 97 of them unidentified.

ஐஐஐஐஐஐஐஐஐஐ

Part Three – World War II

Wakeham, Norman J.

Rank	Regiment	Age at Death
Flying Officer (Nav)	R.A.F. – 166 Squadron	23yrs

Norman John Wakeham was born at Eastbourne in 1921, the son of John and Grace Wakeham. After leaving school, he became a trainee ophthalmic practitioner. He was then living at 162 Whitley Road, in Eastbourne.

He joined the Royal Air Force Volunteer Reserve (*Service No: 160593*) and later served in 166 Squadron, which was a bomber squadron. On 17 July 1943, he returned from his base in Lincolnshire and, at St Mary's Church in Hailsham, he married his childhood sweetheart, Jean Page who was living at 47 Summerheath Road in Hailsham.

He rose to become a Flying Officer (Navigator). 166 Squadron was re-formed for the second time in January 1943 at Kirmington in Lincolnshire where it remained for the rest of the war. The Squadron was mainly flying Wellingtons and Lancasters and participated in many major raids. They also played an active part in 'gardening', which was another name for minelaying. The Lancaster aircraft, of which he was the Navigator, took off to attack Aachen, in Germany on the night of the 27/28th May 1944. On 29th May 1944, Wing Commander D. Garner, wrote to inform his wife that nothing further had been heard of him. He described Norman as a most experienced Navigator. On 17 August, the Air Ministry wrote to inform his wife that German intelligence had been received to say that three identified and three unidentified bodies belonging to his aircraft had lost their lives on 28th May 1944.

Norman was killed in action on 28th May 1944 aged 23 years, only ten months after he had been married. The bodies of the six aircrew were originally buried in the Parish cemetery at Stahe, near Cangelt, approximately 15 miles north of Aachen (*See photo*). After the war, the bodies were re-interred at Reichswald Forest War Cemetery in Germany (*Grave Ref: Coll. Grave 21, C.5-8*).

෴෴෴෴෴෴෴෴෴෴

Part Four – Additional Information

"Additional Information"

This final section provides further information on some of the main events which affected Hailsham men, such as the actions that lead to the award of the Victoria Cross to Nelson Carter and the background to the sinking of HMS "Hood" with such devastating loss of life. Also included are details of the main Memorials abroad commemorating Hailsham men, details of the burials and Memorial Inscriptions in Hailsham Cemetery for both wars and statistics relating to age, rank etc. of the men who died for the town.

Part Four – Additional Information

The ill-fated HMS "Hood" and the Battle of Denmark Strait

HMS "Hood"

HMS "Hood" was the last Britihs battle cruiser of the Royal Navy to be built. She was one of four Admiral-class battlecruisers ordered in mid-1916 under the Emergency War Programme, her design, although drastically revised while she was under construction, still had serious limitations. For this reason, "Hood" was the only one to be constructed. She was named after the 18th-century Admiral, Samuel Hood. When the Spanish Civil War broke out, she was assigned to the Mediterranean Fleet but returned to England in 1939 for an overhaul. At this point "Hood"s usefulness had deteriorated due to changing technology in the naval armour and weaponry. While she was scheduled to undergo a major rebuild in 1941 to correct these issues, the outbreak of the Second World War resulted in her being pressed into service without the upgrades she needed.

When war with Germany was declared in September 1939, "Hood" was operating in the area around Iceland, protecting convoys from German attack. After a brief overhaul to her engine plant, she sailed as the flagship of Force H and, as such, participated in the destruction of the French Fleet at Mers-el-Kebir, intended to deny it from the Germans. Relieved as flagship of Force H she was dispatched to Scapa Flow, and operated in the area as a convoy escort and later as an intercept force against a potential invasion fleet from Germany. In May 1941, she and "Prince of Wales" were ordered to intercept the German battleship "Bismarck" which was en route to attack convoys in the Atlantic.

Part Four – Additional Information

The 'ill-fated' HMS Hood and the Battle of Denmark Strait (contd)

The Battle of the Denmark Strait

When the German battleship, "Bismarck" sailed for the Atlantic in May 1941, "Hood", together with the newly-commissioned battleship "Prince of Wales", was sent out in pursuit, along with several other groups of British capital ships to intercept the German ships before they could break into the Atlantic and attack Allied convoys. "Hood" was commanded by Captain Ralph Kerr and flying the flag of Vice-Admiral Lancelot Holland. The German ships were spotted by two British heavy cruisers on the 23rd May and Holland's ships caught up with "Bismarck" and her consort, the heavy cruiser "Prinz Eugen", in the Denmark Strait between Greenland and Iceland on 24 May.

The British squadron spotted the Germans at 05:37 a.m., but the Germans were already aware of their presence, "Prinz Eugen"'s hydrophones already having detected the sounds of high-speed propellers to their southeast. The British opened fire at 05:52 with "Hood" engaging "Prinz Eugen", the lead ship in the German formation, and the Germans returned fire 05:55, both ships concentrating on "Hood". "Prinz Eugen" (probably) was the first ship to score when a shell hit "Hood"'s boat deck, between her funnels, and started a large fire among the ready-use ammunition for the anti-aircraft guns and rockets of the unrotated projectile mounts. Right before 06:00, while "Hood" was turning 20° to port to unmask her rear turrets, she was hit again on the boat deck by one or more shells from "Bismarck"'s fifth salvo, fired from a range of approximately 16,650 metres (18,210 yd). This same shell, or another from the same salvo, appears to have hit the spotting top as the boat deck was showered with body parts and debris. Almost immediately, a huge jet of flame burst out of "Hood" from the vicinity of the mainmast. This was followed by a devastating magazine explosion that destroyed the after part of the ship. This explosion broke the back of "Hood" and the last sight of the ship, which sank in only three minutes, was her bow, nearly vertical in the water.

Of the 1,418 crew, only 3 men survived. The lucky three were: Signalman Ted Briggs, Midshipman William Dundas and Able seaman Bob Tilburn. They were rescued by the destroyer "Electra" about two and a half hours after the sinking. Four Hailsham men were lost on that fateful day of 24 May 1941: Jack Boniface, Alfred Perrin, Frank Erridge and Kenneth Funnell.

The loss of "Hood" had a profound effect on the British, and the resulting orders from Prime Minister Winston Churchill to the Royal Navy to "*Sink the Bismarck*". This culminated in a naval battle on 26–27 May that ended with the final sinking of the "Bismarck".

ﬠﬠﬠﬠﬠﬠﬠﬠﬠﬠ

Part Four – Additional Information

<u>Company Sergeant Major Nelson V. Carter, VC</u>

The name of Nelson V. Carter, VC, appears on the south face of Hailsham War Memorial and many people must pass by it without giving a second glance. However, they are missing something very special, because the Victoria Cross is the highest award in the Commonwealth for Valour and Bravery. Who was he and what did he do?

Nelson Carter was born on 9th April 1887 at Latimer Road, Eastbourne, the fifth child of Richard and Harriett Carter. Shortly afterwards, the family moved to Harebeating, one of the Brewery (Now Battle) Road cottages in Hailsham (*See photo below*). Nelson was educated at the Hailsham Council Boys School. In December 1902, he enlisted in the Royal Field Artillery originally under an assumed name as he was under age but later under his proper name until he was medically discharged for the second time. He married Cathleen Camfield on 17th October 1911 and set up home at 33 Greys Road, Eastbourne.

In September 1914, Col. Claude Lowther, the owner of Herstmonceux Castle set up recruitment offices all over Sussex and 1,100 men, including Nelson Carter, volunteered within the first two days. Originally designated the 9th Royal Sussex, they became the 11th, the first Southdown Regiment, affectionately known as Lowther's Lambs. By the end of the year, there were three battalions, most of whom came from Sussex. Nelson Carter was attached to A Company, 12th Battalion and was described as being of 'striking appearance', over six feet tall and very muscular.

Following training, the Regiment sailed for France on 4th March 1916 and proceeded to Fleurbaix for further training. On 30th June 1916, Lowther's Lambs took part in, what was described as, a 'diversionary attack' to distract the enemy from the major offensive, the Battle of the Somme, which was due to start the following day. This attack took place at Richebourg L'Avoue, in France. The German position was called the Boar's Head because of its appearance on the trench maps. At 3.05am that morning, following a 15-minute bombardment of German trenches, the 11th, 12th and 13th went '*over the top!*' At the end of this disastrous day, the casualty list was 17 officers and 349 men either killed or missing and over 1000 wounded or taken prisoner. The War Diary shows that they "*bombed and bayoneted their way into enemy lines and beat off repeated counter attacks until they were forced to withdraw as casualties mounted and ammunition ran out*".

Part Four – Additional Information

Company Sergeant Major Nelson V. Carter, VC (Contd)

The battle of Boars Head lasted less than five hours and the 30th June 1916 was later described as 'The Day Sussex Died'. For his actions that day, Sergeant-Major Nelson Victor Carter, aged 29 years, won a posthumous Victoria Cross for exceptional bravery under fire.

His Citation was published in the London Gazette on 9th September 1916. This read as follows.

"For most conspicuous bravery. During an attack, he was in command of the fourth wave of the assault. Under intense shell and machine gun fire, he penetrated with a few men into the enemy's second line and inflicted casualties with bombs. When forced to retire to the enemy's first line, he captured a machine gun and shot the gunner with a revolver. Finally after carrying several wounded men to safety, he was himself mortally wounded and died in a few minutes. His conduct throughout the day was magnificent."

Lieutenant Howard Robinson, Carter's Commanding Officer wrote the following letter to his widow.

"On 30th June, he was in command of the last platoon to go over the parapet. When I last saw him, he was close to the German line, acting as a leader to a small party of four or five men. I was afterwards told that he had entered the German second line and had brought back an enemy machine gun, having put the gun team out of action. I heard that he shot one of them with his revolver. I next saw him about an hour later (I had been wounded in the meanwhile and was lying in our trench). Your husband repeatedly went over the parapet. I saw him going over alone and carrying in our wounded men from 'No Man's Land'. He brought them in on his back, and he could not have done this had he not possessed exceptional physical strength as well as courage. It was in going over for the sixth or seventh time that he was shot in the chest. I saw him fall just inside our trench. Somebody told me that about a month previously your husband carried a man about 400 yards across the open under machine gun fire and brought him safely into our trench. For this act I recommended him for the Military Cross. On every occasion, no matter how tight the hole we were in, he was always cheerful and hopeful, and never spared any pains to make the men comfortable and keep them cheery. In fact, it would be difficult to imagine a man better qualified to lead his comrades into action under the dangerous conditions."

Part Four – Additional Information

<u>Company Sergeant Major Nelson V. Carter, VC (Contd)</u>

King George V wrote to Mrs Carter on 26th March 1917: -

"It is a matter of sincere regret to me that the death of Sergeant-Major Nelson Victor Carter, 12th Battalion Royal Sussex Regiment, deprived me of the pride of personally conferring upon him the Victoria Cross, the greatest of all rewards for valour and devotion to duty."

In May 1917, Mrs Carter received the Victoria Cross from the King on her husband's behalf.

The award of a VC provoked tremendous local sympathy for his widow and six month old daughter, Jessie and a fund was set up. Eastbourne Council gave permission in October 1916 for cinemas in the town to hold benefit performances for the Nelson Carter Memorial Fund. An evening show at the 'Hailsham Electric Cinema' (*The Function Room at the rear of the Corn Exchange*) also helped the fund. By July 1918, the fund reached £472 and provided enough for Jessie's education and also an annuity on her 21st birthday.

Nelson Carter's daughter, Jessie, died a few years ago in Eastbourne. She instructed in her Will that first refusal for ownership of her father's Victoria Cross medal group should go to the Royal Sussex Regiment. The regiment gratefully took up the offer and the VC now resides with the Regimental Museum, based in the Redoubt Fortress at Eastbourne.

A blue plaque was ceremoniously unveiled on 31st July 2007 above No. 33 Greys Road, Eastbourne where Nelson Carter latterly lived. Hugh Wyatt, Lord Lieutenant of West Sussex and president of the Royal Sussex Regiment Association, unveiled the plaque. He remarked: *"He is a very famous son of Eastbourne and it's a good thing to mark the place where he lived"*. Nigel Waterson, the Eastbourne MP was also in attendance and he remarked: *"It is important to pay tribute to this sort of bravery from an earlier generation ….."*. The unveiling ceremony was followed by a reception at the Redoubt Fortress, where the Nelson Carter's medal group is now held.

Company Sergeant-Major Nelson Victor Carter, VC of the 12th Battalion Royal Sussex Regiment was originally buried on the battlefield where he fell but his remains were recovered in the early 1920s and re-interred at the Royal Irish Rifles Graveyard at Laventie, Pas de Calais, France.

Part Four – Additional Information

Coy. Sergeant Major Nelson V. Carter, VC (Contd)

As well as being on the cemetery Memorial at Laventie, he is commemorated on three other War Memorials: – The Regimental chapel of St George in Chichester Cathedral, the Roll of Honour at Eastbourne Town Hall as well as on our own Hailsham Memorial.

Having been brought up and educated at Hailsham, the name of "*C.S.M. Carter, N.V., VC*" appears on the Hailsham Board School 'Roll of Honour'. His name also appears on the Memorial board in St Mary's Parish Church, Hailsham as well as in the 'Roll of Honour' printed earlier in the Parish magazine.

Nelson Victor Carter was born in Eastbourne but brought up in Hailsham which he always considered to be his home town. He was just 29 years old when he died. He was the winner of the Victoria Cross, which is the highest award for valour and bravery. He was also a leader of men and someone of whom we can all be justifiably proud.

The medal group of CSM Carter, VC in the Royal Sussex Regiment Museum at the Redoubt, Eastbourne

囚囚囚囚囚囚囚囚囚囚囚

Part Four – Additional Information

Lowther's Lambs – The South Downs Regiments

The Royal Sussex Regiment was initially raised in 1701 and recruited men locally to fight all over the world. Almost one half of the Hailsham war dead in WW I served with the Royal Sussex Regiment and, of these, nearly one half served with the 11th, 12th and 13th Battalions, referred to as 'Lowther's Lambs'. The reason for this 'Sussex patriotism' is set out in the following brief account.

Colonel Claude Lowther, the son of Captain Francis Lowther, R.N. and second cousin to the fifth Earl of Lonsdale, had previously served with the Imperial Yeomanry in South Africa in 1900, where he was unsuccessfully recommended for the Victoria Cross. He later bought Herstmonceux castle and was the MP for the Eskdale constituency in Cumberland. In September 1914 he received permission from the War Office to raise a battalion of local men. He set up recruitment offices all over Sussex but principally in the seaside towns of Hastings, Bexhill, Eastbourne, Brighton, Worthing and Bognor. Recruitment started on 9th September and within two days, 1100 men had volunteered.

Another Battalion of the Royal Sussex Regiment

In compliance with the desire of the authorities, a special effort is being made to raise another battalion of the Royal Sussex Regiment and it is this battalion which men of the Eastbourne and district recruits will join.

The pay is 1s a day clear. The men are well fed; the war ration includes 1lb of meat a day and plenty of bread, jam and bacon. In the case of a married man, the wife receives 1s a day (7s a week) and 2d a day (1s 2d per week) for each child. Any soldier disabled whilst on active service will enjoy a liberal pension for the rest of his days.

Men between 19 and 35 years of age may join. The standard height is 5ft 9ins and 6ft 3ins; while the chest measurement is 34ins.

LOCAL CENTRES OF INFORMATION

The Eastbourne district has now been divided into four parts (Hailsham, Herstmonceux, Mayfield and Willingdon) and any information may be obtained of the following representatives: -

…..........................

Hailsham – Mr A.K. Burtenshaw

…..........................

(Details taken from a 1914 recruitment advertisement)

Part Four – Additional Information

<u>Lowther's Lambs – The South Downs Regiments (contd)</u>

Originally designated the 9th Royal Sussex, they later became the 11th, the first Southdown Battalion. Because of the 'Southdown' name, they were affectionately known as either 'Lowther's Own' or 'Lowther's lambs'. All original enlistments were given an "SD" (South Downs) prefix to their Regimental number. A further two battalions were raised by the end of the year, the 12th and 13th, most of whom came from Sussex.

Initial training took place at Cooden Camp, near Bexhill before they moved to Detling Camp, near Maidstone in July 1915 when the War Office took direct control. They soon moved to North Camp, Aldershot and in October became part of the 116th Brigade, 39th Division. Training continued until 4th March 1916 when the Regiment sailed for France. They landed at Le Havre and proceeded to Fleurbaix, a front line section in France for instruction and further training. They suffered their first casualty eight days later when a man from Bexhill (David Thomas Dunk) was shot and killed by a sniper. Their first major engagement was  the disastrous 'diversionary' battle of Boar's Head where the casualty list was 17 Officers and 349 men killed or missing with over 1,000 wounded or taken prisoner. This was the day in which three Hailsham heroes lost their lives, Nelson Carter, who won his posthumous VC, David Parsons (1) and Claude Toye.

The South Down battalions subsequently took part in the 1916 Battles of the Somme, such as Fighting on the Ancre (Hamel), Thiepval Ridge etc, the 3rd Battles of Ypres, the 1918 Battles of the Somme and the Battles of the Lys.

ɒɿɒɿɒɿɒɿɒɿ

Part Four – Additional Information

The Memorial Plaque, Memorial Scroll and Letter – WW I

In 1916, it was decided that some form of memorial would be established for presentation to the next of kin of those that died during the war. A government committee was established to decide the nature of this memorial, and in August 1917 it was determined that it would take the form of a bronze plaque, the design of which would be decided by a public competition with a winning prize of £250. The winner was Edward Carter Preston, whose now familiar 4¾ inches diameter (121 mm) 'Memorial Plaque' is illustrated below.

Pictured here is the Memorial Plaque issued for the life of Bert Cox

The selected design was a 12-centimetre disc cast in bronze gunmetal, which incorporated the following;

- Britannia holding an oak spray with leaves and acorns,

- an imperial lion,

- two dolphins representing Britain's sea power,

- the emblem of Imperial Germany's eagle being torn to pieces by another lion,

- a rectangular tablet where the deceased individual's name was cast into the plaque. No rank was given as it was intended to show equality in their sacrifice,

- the words, 'He died for freedom and honour'.

156

Part Four – Additional Information

The Memorial Plaque, Memorial Scroll and Letter – WW I (contd)

The first a family would know of the death of a loved one was the arrival of a telegram from the War Office. This would be followed by the arrival of the Memorial Plaque and then any medals the deceased would have earned by serving his country. The Memorial Plaque would be accompanied by a Memorial Scroll, together with a letter from Buckingham Palace and often a letter from the deceased's commanding officer. They would not usually arrive as a single package, but would come as a series of separate mailings.

The letter from the Palace

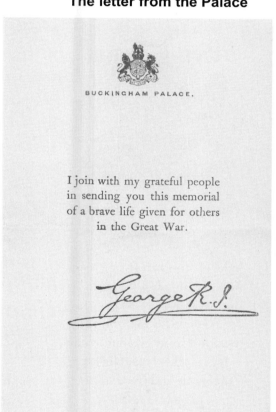

The Memorial Scroll

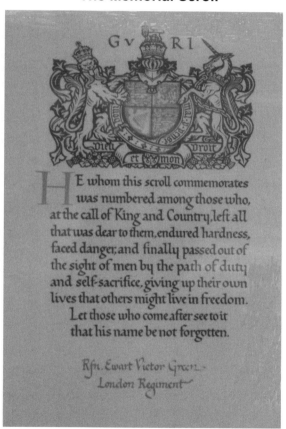

The 'Memorial Plaque' was not popular for obvious reasons and subsequently became referred to as either the 'widow's penny', the 'dead man's penny' or the 'death plaque'.

לּ לּ לּ לּ לּ לּ לּ לּ לּ לּ

Part Four – Additional Information

The Memorial Scroll and Letter – WW II

As happened in the 1st World War, the family would be informed of the death of their loved one by the arrival of a telegram from the War Office. This would be followed by the arrival of the Memorial Scroll together with a letter from Buckingham Palace and often a letter from the deceased's commanding officer. The medals that the deceased would have earned by serving his country were sent separately from the War Office. The 'death plaque', so derided in WW I, did not form part of this 'notification'.

Letter from Buckingham Palace   **The Memorial Scroll**

BUCKINGHAM PALACE

The Queen and I offer you our heartfelt sympathy in your great sorrow.

We pray that your country's gratitude for a life so nobly given in its service may bring you some measure of consolation.

George R.I.

Mrs. A. J. Skinner.

GVI   RI

This scroll commemorates
Leading Aircraftman A. Skinner
Royal Air Force
held in honour as one who
served King and Country in
the world war of 1939-1945
and gave his life to save
mankind from tyranny. May
his sacrifice help to bring
the peace and freedom for
which he died.

Part Four – Additional Information

Gallantry Medals won in World War I

Victoria Cross

Company Sergeant Major **Nelson Carter** of the Royal Sussex Regiment won a posthumous Victoria Cross (**VC**) in June 1916 and the details are given elsewhere. The Victoria Cross is the highest award for valour within the Commonwealth and was instituted in January 1856 by Queen Victoria to honour bravery in the Crimean War. Up to June 2009, it has been awarded to only 1,352 men, three of whom have won it twice (a distinction known as "VC and Bar). It is the most democratic of all medals being open to "every rank and grade of all branches of Her Majesty's forces".

It is a myth that the Victoria Cross is cast from two Russian cannon captured at Sevastopol in the Crimean War. Recent research has shown that the cannons were not Russian but Chinese. An earlier gun was used for the original medals and the Chinese cannon were used from 1914 onwards.

Distinguished Conduct Medal

Second Lieutenant **Frederick Marrillier** of the Royal Sussex Regiment won a posthumous Distinguished Conduct Medal (**DCM**) in October 1914. The 'London Gazette' carried the following announcement: - *"Sergeant (now Second-Lieutenant F.C.J. Marrillier, 2nd Battalion Royal Sussex Regiment) led a party on the night of 1st October and successfully filled one of the enemy's trenches (sic)"*

Sergeant **Alfred Lusted** also of the Royal Sussex Regiment won the Distinguished Conduct Medal (**DCM**) in March 1920. The 'London Gazette' carried the following announcement: - *"For gallantry and devotion to duty, both in the outpost line at Sinjil, Palestine and in France. Especially so in front of Merville in July 1918; he by his daring leadership brought excellent results, including valuable information most helpful to the advance of the battalion."*

The Distinguished Conduct Medal is the oldest British award for gallantry and second only to the Victoria Cross. It is awarded to enlisted personnel, non-commissioned officers and warrant officers of any nation, in any branch of the service, for distinguished conduct in battle.

Part Four – Additional Information

Gallantry Medals won in World War I (Contd)

Military Medal

Sergeant **John Saunders** of the Royal Horse Artillery was awarded the Military Medal **(MM).** This Medal was established in wartime Britain by King George V on 25 March 1916 to be awarded for "acts of gallantry and devotion to duty performed by non-commissioned officers and men of our army in the field". Its inception was intended to meet the enormous demand for medals during the First World War. In a subsequent amendment, women were included whether British subjects or not for "bravery and devotion under fire".The medal was awarded on the recommendation of a Commander-in-Chief in the field. A silver laurelled bar was awarded for subsequent acts of bravery and devotion.

ꗢ ꗢ ꗢ ꗢ ꗢ ꗢ ꗢ ꗢ ꗢ ꗢ

Campaign Medals – WW I

1914 and 1914-15 Stars

The 1914 Star (often called the "Mons Star") was approved by King George V in 1917 for issue to officers and men of British forces who served in France or Belgium between 5th August 1914 and 22nd November 1914. Over 365,000 were issued and the majority of recipients were officers and men of the British Expeditionary Force (*The Old Contemptibles*) who landed in France soon after the outbreak of war and took part in the Retreat from Mons.

The 1914-15 Star was approved in 1918 for issue to officers and men of British and Imperial forces who served in any theatre of war between 5 August 1914 and 31 December 1915. However, it was not given to those who had already qualified for the 1914 Star. The medal and ribbon designs for both Stars are the same apart from the central scroll. The King later approved a clasp, to be worn on the ribbon, to all wearers of the 1914 Star who had actually served under enemy fire during the period concerned.

Part Four – Additional Information

Campaign Medals – WW I (Contd)

1914-1918 British War Medal

The British War Medal 1914 - 1920 was awarded to officers and men of the British and Imperial Forces who had served in uniform or been employed in an "authorised" service and either entered a theatre of war or entered service overseas between 5th August 1914 and 11th November 1918 inclusive. This was later extended to services in Russia, Siberia and some other areas in 1919 and 1920.

Each medal issued was inscribed on the rim with the service number, rank, name and regiment of the recipient. About 6.5 million British War Medals were issued.

Victory Medal

This is a yellow bronze medal, which is also known as the Allied Victory Medal. It was decided that each of the allies should each issue their own bronze Victory medal with a similar design, similar equivalent wording and identical ribbon and was done so as to avoid the mass exchange of medals. The front of the medal depicts a winged classical figure representing peace.

Each medal issued was inscribed on the rim with the service number, rank, name and regiment of the recipient. Approximately 5.7million Victory medals were issued. Not everybody who received the British War Medal also received the Victory medal.

Recipients of either the 1914 or 1914-15 Star also received the British War Medal and Victory Medal. These three medals together were sometimes irreverently referred to as 'Pip, Squeak and Wilfred' (Popular cartoon comic strip characters of the period).

Campaign Medals – WW I (Contd)

Territorial Force War Medal

The Territorial Force War Medal was a campaign medal awarded to members of the British Territorial Force and Territorial Force Nursing Services who served overseas in World War I; it is the rarest of the five British Great War medals.

The medal was established in April 1920 as an award to members of the Territorial Force and Territorial Force Nursing Services who volunteered for service overseas on or before 30 September 1914, and served overseas. They had to:

- have been serving with the force on 4 August 1914, have completed four years service with the force before 4 August 1914 and rejoined the force on or before 30 September 1914

In addition provided that they:

- Undertook, either verbally or by written agreement on or before 30 September 1914 to serve outside the United Kingdom, such agreement being operative after 4 August 1914, and

- Have served outside the United Kingdom between 5 August 1914 and 11 November 1918 (both dates inclusive; note that the last date was in 1918 though the years on the reverse said 1914-19) and

- Did not qualify for the 1914 Star or 1914-15 Star

These campaign medals were struck in bronze and only 33,944 were ever awarded.

ﬔﬔﬔﬔﬔﬔﬔﬔﬔﬔ

Part Four – Additional Information

The main Memorials abroad for Hailsham war deaths

The Menin Gate Memorial, Belgium

The Menin Gate Memorial to the Missing is one of four British and Commonwealth memorials to the missing in the battlefield area of the Ypres Salient in Belgian Flanders. The memorial bears the names of 54,389 officers and men from United Kingdom and Commonwealth Forces (except New Zealand and Newfoundland) who fell in the Ypres Salient before 16th August 1917 and who have no known grave. The Menin Gate, shown on a British Army Trench Map, is on the east side of Ypres. Allied troops leaving the town through this gateway would cross the moat and make their way east into the Ypres Salient battlefields. Many of them would turn right onto the Menin Road.

The names are engraved in Portland Stone panels fixed to the inner walls of the central Hall of Memory, to the sides of the staircases leading from the lower level to the upper exterior level, and on the walls inside the loggias on the north and south sides of the building.

The road leading from the market place to the Menin Gate Memorial is the Meensestraat. This road continues through the Menin Gate Memorial and becomes the Marshalk Frenchlaan. This road is named after Field Marshal Sir John French, who was appointed to the title of 1st Earl of Ypres after the war. He was the first commander of the British Expeditionary Force (B.E.F.) from the time when it landed in France in August 1914 to December 1915. After approximately 150 metres there is a crossroads and, taking the right turn, the road becomes the Meenseweg: the road to Menen. In 1914 Menen was known by its French name of Menin and this road became known to the British Army as "the Menin Road".

The following Hailsham soldiers are commemorated on this Memorial:

Brook, James	Knight, Charles
Maryan, Ernest	Marillier, Frederick
Ripley, Abraham (1)	Noakes, Percy

ꄱꄱꄱꄱꄱꄱꄱꄱꄱꄱ

Part Four – Additional Information

The main Memorials abroad for Hailsham war deaths (Contd)

The Thiepval Memorial, France

The Thiepval Memorial to the missing of the Somme, bears the names of more than 72,000 officers and men of the United Kingdom and South African forces who died in WW1 in the Somme sector before 20th March 1918 and have no known grave. Over 90 percent of those commemorated are those who died between July and November 1916. The memorial also serves as an Anglo-French Battle Memorial in recognition of the joint nature of the Somme 1916 offensive and a small cemetery containing equal numbers of Commonwealth and French graves lies at the foot of the memorial.

On 1st July 1916, supported by a French attack to the south, thirteen divisions of Commonwealth forces launched an offensive on a line from north of Gommecourt to Maricourt. Despite a preliminary bombardment lasting seven days, the German defences were barely touched and the attack met unexpectedly fierce resistance. Losses were catastrophic and with only minimal advances on the southern flank, the initial attack was a failure.

In the following weeks, huge resources of manpower and equipment were deployed in an attempt to exploit the modest successes of the first day. However, the German Army resisted tenaciously and repeated attacks and counter attacks meant a major battle for every village, copse and farmhouse gained. At the end of September 1916, the village of Thiepval was finally captured. The village had been an original objective of the 1st July 1916 Somme offensive. Attacks north and east continued throughout October and into November 1916 in increasingly difficult weather conditions. The Battle of the Somme finally ended on 18th November 1916 with the onset of winter.

> The following Hailsham soldiers are commemorated on this Memorial:
>
> Atkins, Ernest   Milward, Frank
> Saunders, Charles   Smith, John

꙲꙲꙲꙲꙲꙲꙲꙲꙲꙲

Part Four – Additional Information

The main Memorials abroad for Hailsham war deaths (Contd)

Le Touret Memorial, France

The Le Touret Memorial is located at the east end of Le Touret Military Cemetery, Richebourg-L'Avoue, Pas-de-Calais, France. Over 13,000 names are listed on the Memorial of Commonwealth soldiers (Canadian and Indian troops excepted) who fell in the fighting from October 1914 until 24th September 1915, prior to the Battle of Loos on 24th September 1915.

The memorial is located in the grounds of Le Touret Military Cemetery, Festubert. It takes the form of a loggia surrounding an open rectangular court. The court is enclosed by three solid walls and on the eastern side by a colonnade. East of the colonnade is a wall, and both are prolonged to the north and south, forming a long gallery where nearly half the names are listed. The stone for this memorial came from Nimes.

The following Hailsham soldiers are commemorated on this Memorial:

Hollebon, Charles   Smith, George
Rigglesford, Edgar

෴෴෴෴෴෴෴෴෴෴

Part Four – Additional Information

Statistics (for those named on the memorial)

Places of Death/Burial	WW I	WW II
Belgium	16	1
France	46	5
Germany	2	5
Other Countries	4	9
UK - Hailsham	13	2
UK – Other Towns	3	3
At Sea / Drowned	3	9
Air Crash - Unknown	0	1
Unknown	1	0

1. As would be expected, in WW1, virtually three quarters of the deaths/burials occurred in France and Belgium where the main battles, such as the Somme and Ypres, took place.

2. The number of deaths/burials in 'Other Countries' in WW2 highlights the wider range and greater coverage of that war – Sicily 2; Singapore 1; Libya 1; Luxembourg 1; Italy 3; Netherlands 1.

Ages at Death	WW I	WW II
20 years and under	12	8
21years to 25 years	30	8
26 years to 30 years	20	8
31 years and over	24	11
Unknown	2	0
Youngest	18 years	18 years
Oldest	47 years	65 years

1. In WW I, 42 out of the 86 deaths (where the ages are known) were 25 years or younger. In WW II, this figure was 16 out of 35. The percentage of 'young men' who died in WW I was clearly far higher than in WW II.

2. The oldest person to be killed was Harry Sea-Mays, at age 65, a merchant seaman in WW II. It had not been possible to identify exactly who is the youngest person named on the Memorial as there are several contenders.

Part Four – Additional Information

Statistics (for those named on the Memorial)

Rank/Officer Status	WW I	WW II
Commissioned Officers	5	3
Warrant Officers	1	1
Non Commissioned Officers (NCOs)	16	18
Other Ranks	64	13
No Rank (Merchant Navy) or Unknown	2	0

It is interesting to compare the numbers in the different classes of ranks. Taking into account the difference in overall numbers, 88 as against 35, there were a far lower number of NCOs in WW I and far more 'Other Ranks' mainly because of the way in which the wars were fought.

Regiment (Initial Choice)	WW I
Royal Sussex (Lowther's Lambs)	13
Royal Sussex (Other Battalions)	29
Royal Field/Horse Artillery	10
London	5

In ww1, many of the soldiers were transferred to different Regiments from their initial choice. This might have been because of their particular expertise or, more likely, because of the carnage that occurred, that many Regiments (or what was left of them) were merged with the remains of others. In WW II, except for the four who served on HMS "Hood", only a few were in the same Regiment as anyone else and no-one was in the same Squadron as anyone else. No statistics are therefore given.

Service Chosen	WW I	WW II
Army (WW II includes tank, parachute etc)	84	19
Royal/Merchant Navy	4	10
Royal Flying Corps/Royal Air Force	0	6
Unknown	0	0

As is clearly illustrated, advancing technology between the First and Second World Wars rapidly changed the nature of warfare.

Part Four – Additional Information

<u>Extract from a letter dated 29 September 1944 sent from France by Captain R.A. Helsdon, who was an administrator in the European Civil Affairs Regiment</u>

.... Altogether I have had a mighty interesting time since I came over and I am very glad that I joined up as I did. After landing in Normandy, we remained for nearly six weeks in various 'pools' waiting our chance to work, but during that time I was able to get about quite a bit to study conditions. I visited Cherbourg, Caen, Bayeaux, etc. Then came the big American advance and we really got moving. Incidentally I had a front seat view of the 3,000 plane raid that started the big advance and it was a sight that I will never forget.

Then we travelled fast, we went straight across France, through Versailles, Paris, Chateau Thierry etc and into Belgium. Our first really big job was

taking over a very big Belgium city on the same day as the Germans left. It was simply terrific. We were pelted with flowers, kissed by thousands and nearly drowned in champagne, cognac etc etc. We worked like the blazes for a week and did some good work. Then we moved on and have been very busy ever since. I can claim the questionable honour of having started the first German Refugee Camp of this war. I have now handed over that job but it was very interesting.

It has not been easy in France and Belgium administering civil affairs because one had to be careful to emphasise that we were 'Liberators' and not taking over the government. But I find proper military government much easier as we are the boss and the Jerries have to jump to it. I got a terrific kick out of crossing the German Frontier for the first time. One job I had which gave me a lot of pleasure was in our last village. The German soldiers had occupied a big school building and before they left, they did as much damage as they could and messed in most of the rooms. It pleased me a lot to make the German civilians clean and scrub it all out for them to occupy themselves as a refugee camp. There is no doubt that I have been able to see a lot more than the average soldier. ....

卐卐卐卐卐卐卐卐卐卐

Part Four – Additional Information

Burials in Hailsham Cemetery of WW I men not named on War Memorial

Commonwealth War Graves

Belcher, William Henry – Private, South Wales Borderers (*Service No:3/1307*) – Died 9th January 1918 aged 23 years at 1 Sharp Street, Widnes (*Grave space No. 1635*)

Burgess, Gilbert Moy – Able Seaman (*Service No: J/40911*) HMS "Cleopatra" - Drowned at sea 9th November 1920 aged 21 years - HMS "Cleopatra"; brought back from Plymouth (*Grave space No. 1349*)

Harding, Henry – Pioneer, Royal Engineers (*Service No: 92343*) – Died on 3rd May 1916 aged 31 years at Railway Cottage, High Street, Polegate (*Grave space No. 1591*)

Huggett, Harry – Private, Royal Defence Corps (*Service No:73337*) - Died 9th November 1918 aged 38 years at the Military Hospital, Cork (*Grave space No. 1547*)

Putland, Albert Edmund – Corporal, Royal Sussex Regiment (*Service No: G/1930*) – Died 14th July 1916 aged 26 years at the 2nd Birmingham War Hospital (*Grave space No. 1588*)

Private/Family Graves

Baker, James – Aged 35 – Able-bodied seaman who died on 20th March 1917 at the East Sussex County Asylum, Hellingly – No headstone (*Grave space No. 1223*)

Page, Richard Charles – Aged 18 years – Stoker, Royal Navy – Died 22nd September 1918 at the Royal Navy Barracks, Portsmouth (*Grave space No. 474*)

Penwell, Francis George – Aged 20 years – Private, 13th Middlesex Regiment – Died 16th April 1917 at St Bartholomews Hospital, London (*Grave space No. 1629*)

ꙮꙮꙮꙮꙮꙮꙮꙮꙮꙮ

Part Four – Additional Information

Burials in Hailsham Cemetery of WW II men not named on War Memorial

Commonwealth War Graves

Haller, Arthur C. - Gunner, Royal Artillery (*Service No: H08466*) – Died 22nd September 1942 aged 23 years (*Grave space No: 3221*)

Mayhew, Frederick E. W. – Pilot Officer, Royal Air Force – Died 17th May 1944 aged 31 years (*Grave space No: 3113*)

Moore, Frederick J. – Motor Mechanic (Leading Rate), Royal Navy (*Service No: C/MX 550303*) – Died 13th May 1944 aged 19 years (*Grave space No: 3428*)

Oliver, Lancelot F. – Aircraftman, Royal Air Force (*Service No: 460709*) – Died 14th December 1943 aged 38 years (*Grave space No: 3220*)

Pollock-Gore, William A.J. - Lieutenant, 20th Sussex Battalion Home Guard – Died 20th February 1944 aged 46 years (*Grave space No: 2522*)

Private/Family Graves

Nil

囧囧囧囧囧囧囧囧囧囧

Part Four – Additional Information

Memorial Inscriptions in Hailsham Cemetery to WW I deaths
not named on War Memorial

Brown, George Albert – Eldest son of the above (*George William and Frances Brown*) who fell in France August 21st 1918 (*Grave space 472*)

Charles, Richard – Died June 23rd 1918 aged 38 of the Royal Engineers, also …. (*Grave space No. 1202*)

Colbran, E – Sapper, died of wounds received in the Battle of Neuve Chapelle March 29, 1915 aged 20 (*Son of Mary Ann Colbran*) (*Grave space 1530*)

Hastings, Alfred Howard – Died in France 1918 aged 31 (*Son of Alfred and Martha Hastings*) (*Grave space 594*)

Jarvis, Albert George – Died of wounds 12th September 1917 aged 19 years – Interred at Outtersteene, France (*Son of Frank and Mildred Jarvis*) (*Grave space 2379*)

Manser, George - Private 41299 D Coy. Norfolk Regiment – Missing, presumed killed April 10th 1918, aged 29 (*Grave space 7395*)

Stenning, Ambrose Nelson - R.A.C.A., (*son of Ambrose Stenning*) killed in action in France March 25th 1916 aged 26 years (*Grave space 415*)

Tassell, Bertram T. – Rifleman, London Regiment; Killed in action April 14th 1917 aged 34 years (*Grave space 1074*)

ꕔꕔꕔꕔꕔꕔꕔꕔꕔꕔ

Memorial Inscriptions in Hailsham Cemetery to WW II deaths
not named on War Memorial

King, Frank – Killed in France 1940 (*Son of Charles and Charlotte King*) (*Grave space No: 2444*)

Richards, Albert – Presumed killed in action on 29th May 1941 in Crete (*Grave space No: 3509*)

ꕔꕔꕔꕔꕔꕔꕔꕔꕔꕔ

Acknowledgements

The author wishes to express his sincere thanks to the following people in particular for their help, mainly in providing information and photographs for this book but others for their overall assistance in many other ways.

Adams, Colin	King, Mr B.
Atkins, Stuart	Kitcher, Mrs Maxine
Attree, Rose	Lavender, Eric & Una
Bennett, Brian	Lelliott, David
Brook, Peter	Lester, David
Bruce, Bob	Matt (Michelham Priory)
Burgess, John & Peggy	Mitchell, Brian
Cousens, Ronnie	Morris, Bob
Deacon, Des & Sheila	Parks, Alison
Duffell, Brenda	Payne, Tom
Ellis, Mrs Margaret	Pettigrew, Martin
Fuller, Ann & Ron	Pettigrew, Vince & Marianne
Funnell, Barry	Phair, Arden
Funnell, Mrs	Pollard, Graham
Goldsmith, Brian & Doreen	Pye, Roger
Hailsham Historical & Natural History Society	Richardson, Amanda
	Ridley, Harry
Hailsham Town Council – <u>All staff</u>	Saunders, Jean & John
Harris, Mr & Mrs	Small, Mrs P.
Helsden, David	Smith, Les
Hillman, Alan	Talbot, Carol
Hollebon, Robert	Taylor, Richard

The author also wishes to acknowledge the kind assistance of the many other people who have provided either snippets of information or helpful comments along the way, all of which have been invaluable in helping with the compilation of this book.